Flight Path

A biography of Frank Barker Jr.

For the last three decades, I have considered Frank Barker one of the outstanding pastors in America. His ministry at Briarwood Presbyterian Church in Birmingham, a church he founded, has reached out to every part of the world. I highly recommend this book to young pastors because it will enrich their ministry. They will discover the central ingredients of the Christian life and how to have a missions program that will be a blessing to the entire world. I thank God for Frank Barker.

The Late Bill Bright, Founder and Chairman,
Campus Crusade for Christ

Most biographies should be burned! That is because most biographies exalt the greatness of a servant and nobody should worship at the altar of anybody except God. This is a biography you should keep and one you should read and re-read. It tells me about a servant, Frank Barker, but it points to Christ on every page. As I've read this book, I've laughed and I've cried and I've rejoiced in its honesty and reality but, far more than that, I've seen Christ and what He will do through His servants who will do it His way. Read this book! You'll be so glad you did.

Steve Brown,
Reformed Theological Seminary, Orlando, Florida

The story of Frank Barker is an amazing account of how God uses the faithful and the humble. In a marvelous way Christ sought him, saved him, and made him an effective instrument for the building up of the church. What a remarkable and encouraging legacy! May God bless this book to the edification of many readers. "Be steadfast and unmovable, always abounding in the work of the Lord; you know that your labor in Him is not in vain" (1 Cor. 15:58).

John MacArthur, Senior Pastor,
Grace Community Church, Los Angeles, California

The book kept me spellbound! The only time I have to read is at bedtime and I couldn't wait for that time to come, and then I couldn't quit reading! Frank's ministry parallels ours so much. I appreciate the opportunity to read the manuscript.

Anne Kennedy (Mrs. D. James Kennedy)

Janie Buck having applied her skills to share the testimony of my good friend and home pastor, Frank Barker, should result in thousands being blessed in a phenomenal way. At long last the story of this humble man who built one of the leading churches in this country is being told. Frank's simple life of faith in a supernatural God who delights in doing the impossible when we trust Him should warm your heart, and hopefully be an example to many. I was spiritually refreshed as I relived some of the experiences related in this wonderful book.

**Bailey Marks, Senior Vice President,
Campus Crusade for Christ**

What an extraordinary privilege to recommend this book on one of the great pastors that our Lord has provided for His church, Dr. Frank Barker. Frank has been my mentor, my friend, and now my colleague as he serves as Pastor Emeritus of Briarwood where I have had the privilege to follow him into the role of Senior Pastor. At that church the Lord used him to establish and grow with the mission to "reach Birmingham to reach the world for Christ." This book will give you insights on how the extraordinary power of God works through a man who has an extraordinary commitment to serve His God.

**Harry Reeder, Senior Pastor,
Briarwood Presbyterian Church, Birmingham,
Alabama**

One of the great American pastors of the twentieth century, Dr. Frank Barker's dramatic conversion and selfless service translated into a remarkable ministry that touched thousands of lives and made a major contribution to international missions. If I were to select a model pastor, Frank Barker would be that person. I am thrilled that his life story is now available so that more people can become acquainted with this gifted man of God and the global vision that marked his ministry at Briarwood Presbyterian Church.

Luder G. Whitlock, Jr., Excelsis

This is the page-turning story of one of the most remarkable ministers of the Gospel I have ever known. When I think of Frank Barker the words that come first to mind are faithfulness and humility. His love for God's Word and his desire to share the Gospel with everyone everywhere are the consuming passions of his life. I wish that every young minister could spend a year under the tutelage of Frank Barker. A great read about a mighty man of God!

Timothy George
Dean, Beeson Divinity School of Samford
University, Birmingham, Alabama

Early in my ministry, I spent several days with Frank, following him around and watching everything he did to learn all I could from him. Besides his commitment to prayer and his heart for evangelism, the other obvious fact about Frank's life and ministry was how hard he worked daily from early until late. The Lord greatly blessed Frank's diligence as well as his faithfulness.

Robert C. Cannada, Jr.
President , Reformed Theological Seminary

Flight Path

A biography of Frank Barker Jr.

Janie Buck and Mary Lou Davis

CHRISTIAN FOCUS

About the Authors

Janie Buck, wife and mother of two children and six grand-children, is a Bible teacher and speaker. She and husband Dr. William P. Buck worked part time with Campus Crusade for Christ for 30 years. They are teachers and mentors in Briarwood Presbyterian Church. Together they teach seminars and lead retreats. Janie has authored four other books and numerous articles. She explores matters of faith on web site www.insightstofaith.com.

Mary Lou Davis is their daughter and co-author. Along with writing for youth, she is a photographer. Her photographs have appeared in major magazines. For fifteen years, she and husband Dusty were on staff with Athletes in Action, a division of Campus Crusade. Presently, they work with campus Out Reach, a college ministry of Briarwood. They have three children.

ISBN 1-85792-918-7 Paperback
ISBN 1-85792-932-2 Hardback

© Copyright Janie Buck 2003
Published in 2003
by
Christian Focus Publications, Ltd.
Geanies House, Fearn, Tain,
Ross-shire, IV20 1TW, Great Britain.
www.christianfocus.com

Cover Design by Alister MacInnes

Printed and bound by
MacKay's of Chatham

Contents

Foreword

I first laid eyes on Frank Barker about forty-six years ago as I was sitting in a theology classroom at Columbia Theological Seminary in Atlanta, Georgia. He was sitting in the back row with his chair tilted back, leaning against the wall, with a look of total bewilderment on his face. I didn't know at the time that he had arrived in seminary without ever coming to know the gospel or the meaning of salvation. Seminary was hard enough for a Christian, and for one whose eyes had not yet been opened to understanding spiritual things, it must have been totally incomprehensible. I could not have imagined at that time that this befuddled young man, in just a few months, was going to grasp the gospel, be completely transformed and go on to become one of the most effective ministers in the United States. But that is getting ahead of the story.

Though Frank had grown up in a church, by the time he went to college and then into the Naval Air Corps, he had pretty well jettisoned the principles that he had learned as a child, as so many other young people have done before and since. If he had grasped the gospel in those early years the next decade of his life would have been far different. But at that point he did not have ears to hear.

The story that the author tells so engagingly about his college career and his life flying jet planes off of carriers is often hair-raising. Over and over again he was rescued from the very precipice of death by God, who was evidently preserving his life for far greater things.

This was to come to a climax when after a weekend

of carousing, he was driving back to Pensacola Air Base along one of those deserted Alabama highways near the Florida border, when he went to sleep while traveling sixty miles per hour. The highway turned and he didn't. He found himself flying down a dirt road with trees flashing by on either side. He finally brought the car to a halt a few inches from a large pine tree on which was a sign that was to dramatically change his life.

It was not too long after that that he left the Naval Air Corps and came to seminary in order to make his life more pleasing to God. Having, after a few months, discovered the incredible good news of the grace of Christ and the free gift of eternal life, he went on to finish his education and then was called to Birmingham, Alabama, to start a new church. From that tiny beginning, through the indefatigable labors of Frank and his wife, Barbara, over a period of about forty years, was developed one of the great mega-churches of America.

This biography written so enthrallingly by authors Janie Buck and Mary Lou Davis, is filled with innumerable lessons in life. Lessons in what it means to be a humble servant of Christ; of what it means to live a life which is unquestionably totally dedicated to God; of what it means to forge, after a rocky beginning, a marriage which is genuinely a partnership in love; of what it means to rear godly children in the midst of an incredibly busy schedule; of what it means to trust God for all your daily needs while giving away the preponderance of your income to the work of Christ; of what it means to live for the glory of Christ in the midst of the accolade of this world.

I do not believe that anyone can read this exciting and moving story of lives lived for the kingdom of God without becoming a better person through the experience.

Fascinatingly written in the first person, it is a story reminiscent of the famous book by Catherine Marshall entitled A *Man Called Peter*. In my opinion, this, too, would make a marvelous motion picture.

D. James Kennedy, Ph.D.
Senior Minister, Coral Ridge Presbyterian Church

Acknowledgments

There was no way we could record all the great things God did in and through the life of Frank Barker. After two years of collecting information and praying, God led us to write as if Frank was writing his own story. Nearly everything he has said was either recorded on audio tape or written in his typed sermons. He also provided ample pages of documentation to questions about events we were unsure of. Therefore not much literary license was taken.

My daughter, Mary Lou Buck Davis, came to my aid when I was overwhelmed with the task. She worked side-by-side with me adding much needed organization to the chapters. We had help from our husbands, Dr. William Pettus Buck and James Earnest (Dusty) Davis. They were our best critics and first editors. Cliff Cox, an old friend, helped correct many of our mistakes, as did Tom Harris and Tom Bradford. We are thankful for their help. And Peggy Barker Townes gave time and added corrections. Kelly Issacson Buck, my precious daughter-in-law, did major editing. Of course, Frank scoured the manuscript thoroughly to correct facts. All of us who worked on the manuscript benefited and learned to trust God more from the lessons He taught Frank and Barbara.

Ten necessary things to stay alive

Get my head back or I'll snap my neck. Pull my elbow into my stomach or I'll pull the stick back and spin in. Take my feet off the brakes or I'll blow both tires and can't land.

I sat in the ready room of the aircraft carrier waiting for my plane's turn to be catapulted off the deck. My mind was racing to remember the ten things necessary for me to stay alive. This was my first time to be catapulted off a carrier and I could remember only nine of the ten things!

"Barker! Man your plane!" shouted a voice over the squawk box. I grabbed my helmet, clanked down the metal stairs taking two at a time and jumped into the cockpit.

Six of the crew pushed my jet backward onto the narrow platform elevator that would raise it to the flight deck. I hated this part. It felt like I was hanging in space off the side of the ship, with no railing to keep my million dollar plane (with its nice pilot) from crashing into the sea below.

At the whistle I stepped on the brakes. Unexpectedly, the jet lurched backward. Carriers always launch aircraft into the wind. The ship was traveling at around 33 knots, so there was a 40 to 50 knot wind coming down that deck. That wind surged under my left wing violently, lifting the nose of the plane into the air.

I gasped, leaning forward as if to counterbalance the plane. I saw terror in the eyes of the sailors in front of me, and knew there were only moments before I would career over the edge of the carrier. One of the crew jumped up and grabbed the nose wheel. The plane lurched back to the deck. I exhaled heavily, not realizing till then I had been holding my breath.

Everyone resumed his position as if nothing had happened, and the elevator began to whine as it lifted me to the flight deck. I was shook, but in my mind I started rehearsing the list of ten things I needed to remember. I counted them out, murmuring to myself as I turned up my engines, and taxied to the catapult.

"Ready?" the officer signaled to me.

Everything is timed on an aircraft carrier. Every twenty five seconds a plane is supposed to take off. Right catapult fires. Jet positioned on the left, then left catapult fires. It's the catapult officer's job to get the jet launched, but he can't "shoot you" till you salute.

Take my feet off the brakes or I will blow both tires and can't land... I could only remember nine things. What was the tenth! The catapult officer kept signaling impatiently. I was throwing off his perfect timing. What was that last thing? I put my head back and saluted anyway.

Bam! The G forces pulled on my body as the catapult launched me across the deck. Number ten came back to me with frightening clarity. A little metal bar had to be pulled up and gripped with the throttle when the plane is catapulted. If not, the jet will be thrown off the ship, but the throttle will come off and the pilot will not have enough power to get airborne.

In a panic I jammed the throttle up. Too late! I shot off the deck and dropped like lead.

If a plane goes into the water, the next thing that happens is the aircraft carrier runs over you. I could hear my engines building, but I wasn't getting enough power.

In a prop plane you get immediate power, but in a jet, once you get below a certain percent, you can push the throttle up, but nothing will happen. I thought flying was the ultimate freedom. My life flashed before my eyes.

2

Free-wheeling

High school brought my first taste of freedom. With my driver's license and the family car, I could go wherever I wanted. I joined a high school fraternity whose favorite pastime was driving through Birmingham at night hurling eggs and obscenities at people. Revving my engine, I would carefully time the traffic light to make our getaway. It wasn't that I really liked doing this, but I was driven by a desire to be accepted by the boys. I went along with the crowd.

One Friday night the frat brothers threw a big party. I had started drinking and didn't know when to stop. Heading home, I hoped Mother wouldn't be waiting up for me. As I drove the deserted streets, I dreaded seeing her. Maybe I could hold my breath so she wouldn't smell alcohol.

Turning out the car lights, I coasted into the driveway. As I tiptoed up the front steps, I remembered I hadn't oiled the hinges on the front door. I opened the door one inch at a time, trying not to let it squeak, went in and carefully closed it. I had made it!

Turning around slowly to head to my room, I came up short. Mom was standing right in front of me. Tears streamed down her face. She didn't have a switch in her hand like she used to when I was a kid, but I wished she had. It would have been easier to take than this.

She whispered fiercely, "Son, you're killing your father by the way you are living!"

"I'm sorry, Mother," I stammered. "I'll try to do better." It was a hollow promise. I genuinely wanted to please her, but the pull of my friends was stronger.

It wasn't much later that I came home from another big party. I had some whiskey left and devised a great plan to hide the bottle in my coat pocket in order to slip it into the house.

Dad's bedroom was at the foot of the stairs. I knew he'd be awake because he usually waited up for me. Thinking I could avoid him, I took off my shoes and tiptoed toward the staircase. Halfway across the entrance hall, I saw him in his room. He was on his knees. I didn't have to guess for whom he was praying.

He looked up, "Come here, Frank."

"Yes, sir." I walked resignedly into his room.

With a sadness I had never before seen in his eyes he asked, "Let me see your coat."

The excitement of the evening turned bitter in my mouth. Dang! How had he known? I hated disappointing my Dad. There was no escape. I felt sick to my stomach. Ashamed, I handed him the coat.

Reaching directly into the inside pocket, he found the bottle. He pulled it out and held it up in front of me. I stammered an apology. Again, I promised to try to do better.

In spite of all my good intentions, I kept running wild with my fraternity brothers. I usually crept up the stairs to my room at two or three o'clock in the morning. Guilt hung over me like a cloud. I knew that what I was doing was wrong but couldn't seem to change myself. When it came right down to it, I didn't really want to change.

One afternoon I came home from school to news that did sober me. My father had suffered a heart attack and was on the verge of death at the hospital.

3

One of the boys

I knew Mother was right. My actions had attacked his heart. It sobered me to see my strong father lying weak and pale in the hospital bed. I believed I had been the cause of it. I was killing him with my behavior. It made me determined to quit living on the wild side.

My father loved God. He was an elder at church. He would stand at the door of the church and greet people as they came in. He would say, "I shake them in, the deacons shake them down, and the preacher shakes them out."

When Dad came home from the hospital, I again took part in our family devotions, even getting on my knees and praying with my parents. I never doubted the truth about God and the Bible, but it didn't affect my life.

When I was younger, I went to the "Wonderbook Camp." It was something two unmarried, middle-aged ladies in our church did for the local kids. Renting a campsite in the state park near Birmingham for a week in the summers, they rounded up as many kids as they could and bussed them out there.

On the last night we sat around the crackling fire watching the sparks fly up into the darkness. We sang the camp songs and listened to a final "sermon." The leader invited us to give our lives to the Lord. That sounded like a good thing to do, so along with most of the other kids, I dedicated my life to Christ. But when I came home, there was no change in my life. It had just been an emotional experience.

It never occurred to me to question going to church. That's what all good people did in the South. I believed everything I heard at church. Sunday mornings I would get up and go to the Presbyterian church with my parents. During the break between the church service and Sunday school, I walked down the block to King's Drugstore. If I didn't have any money, I simply stole a candy bar to munch on the short walk back to church.

In spite of all my good intentions to change my life, when a friend came knocking, I was out the door drinking and gambling again. Why couldn't I change? To protect my parents I resolved to at least be more secretive.

One fall Saturday morning I awoke with the warm Indian summer sun streaming into my bedroom window. I rolled over and looked at the clock. It was already 11:00. Shaking sleep off, I was aware of a commotion outside. I stumbled over to look out of my bedroom window, and to my horror, there was a police car on the curb!

That jolted me awake. I ducked behind the curtain. "They got me!" Panic gripped my stomach as I tried to remember what I had done the night before. I had been drinking a lot and couldn't remember what I had done.

Slowly, I pulled on my pants and T-shirt. I knew I had to face them. I walked barefoot down the stairs wondering why mother hadn't come to get me.

Mother had her back to me and was looking out the window when I came down. As casually as I could I asked, "What are the police doing outside?"

She turned and faced me.

Oh no, here it comes. I cringed.

"They are responding to a problem across the street. I'm not sure what's going on," she said, turning back to the window.

I tried to look concerned but wanted to laugh. Relief was sweet.

My senior year the brothers elected me treasurer of the fraternity. That was a heady job. Once, my position came in handy when I couldn't pay a gambling debt. I didn't want my folks to find out. I believed the fraternity owed me for working so hard to keep up with all the money. No one will ever know, I thought, as I "borrowed" twenty-five dollars. If I had known what embarrassment that debt would cause me later, I'm not sure I would have taken it.

My grades weren't too bad considering the little thought I gave to studying. Graduation is the peak of an eighteen year old's life. When the high school annuals came out, everyone looked for his picture to read what the editors had written about them. There was "Most Likely to Succeed," "Most Beautiful," "Most Intelligent" and other nice things written under each picture. Under my name was "One of the Boys." That's exactly the way I wanted it. I didn't want to be different.

4

Turning my face to the sky

College provided the freedom I had longed for. Now I would be free to act however I wanted, without fear of getting caught, or giving my Dad another heart attack. I got a Naval ROTC scholarship to Alabama Polytechnic Institute, which later became Auburn University. In spite of Auburn's "good moral influence," I continued down the path I had begun in high school.

I won a spot on the university tennis team. The coach kept close tabs on the player and I didn't want a hangover hampering my game, so I was on my best behavior during competitions. After a tournament in Mississippi with Ole Miss, I returned to my apartment to see the windows knocked out and the door ripped off the hinges.

My immediate response was, "Man! I must have missed a great party!" I felt better when I learned a tornado had touched down on campus. I had not missed a good party.

A few of my college fraternity brothers were strong Christians. I respected them, but not enough to want to be like them. Although I still believed in God, I quit going to church unless I went home to Birmingham. Sundays became recovery days from Saturday night binges.

God was like a safety net I'd run to if I needed something. I'll never forget the night I drove out of Auburn into the country, which isn't very far. I found a large field where I hoped no one could see me praying. If anyone had seen me, he wouldn't have believed it was Frank Barker.

The sky was lit by a million stars and I knew God was out there somewhere. I knew He listened when people prayed because I had seen answers when my parents prayed. I made sure no-one was driving down that road, then switched off the car lights. The night was so still, except for the crickets and katydids. A whippoorwill's lonesome song came from a nearby tree. I climbed over the barbed wire fence, walked way out into the field and fell down on my knees. "Oh God," I said turning my face to the sky, "I'm in big trouble. I've really messed up with my girlfriend. If you get me out of this mess, I promise I'll never do that again." I looked up at the stars and knew that God would help me. I thought I was a Christian. After all, I did go to church sometimes. Maybe God would listen to me because my Dad prayed for me. He wrote every week to tell me he was praying for me. His prayers gave me confidence that God was watching out for me.

God did answer that prayer, and I was relieved to find my worst nightmare was over. However, before a month passed, I forgot the promise I made to God and went back to my same old habits. That was the pattern of my college years.

Because I was on a Navy scholarship, I served each summer as a midshipman. One summer I was on the battleship USS Wisconsin. We sailed to France and my buddies and I went to all the famous French girlie shows. These were more pornographic than anything I had previously been involved with. When my friends hired prostitutes, I drew the line. I thought, *I'm OK, but those guys are really bad off.*

Back at the university that fall, my fraternity brothers and I started going to Phenix City, a town near Auburn that was notoriously filled with gambling and strip clubs.

It was at that time that one of my friends started dating a high school girl from Birmingham named Barbara Brown. She was a knockout! I thought, *If he ever breaks up with her, I'm going to ask her out.* Then I thought, *I'm going to ask her out whether he breaks up with her or not.* I never got around to asking her out then, but I knew someday she would be mine.

At the outbreak of the Korean War, my ROTC training went from just playing war to a very serious training regimen. I knew it wouldn't be long before we would be shot at by real bullets. Our training would be tested and death would be waiting for any mistake.

5

Death became a companion

Upon graduation I went on active duty as an officer in the Navy. I applied for flight training, but there was a backlog of men ahead of me. In the meantime, I was sent to a destroyer in the North Atlantic. The seas were very rough and everyone on the ship got seasick. But the Navy doesn't care how much you are throwing up. You have to continue your duties, sick or not. It was hard to drag myself out of my bunk and stumble through that lurching hunk of metal to carry out my orders.

Eight months later I was glad to be off that ship and headed for flight training. I bought a very used Studebaker and drove from Birmingham to the Naval Air Station at Pensacola, Florida. Checking into the barracks, I wasn't surprised at how spartan they were. I never expected it to be otherwise.

My room-mate was as wild as I was, and we immediately hit it off. He was Roman Catholic and always got up Sunday morning to go to confession. I slept in.

Our initial training was at "Mainside." There, we went through ground school, learning about aerodynamics and flight principles. Then we went to an outlying field to begin flight training.

I'll never forget my first flight. The airplane trainer was an SNJ, a yellow, single-engine, propeller-driven plane with two cockpits. The student sat in front, the instructor in back.

My instructor was a tough marine named Captain Tope. He took me on my first flight. At one point he said, "Now I'm going to demonstrate a stall spin. Follow me through it on your controls and see how we get into it and how we get out. If we are not out by two and a half spins, bail out!"

With that statement I started to quake. He pulled the nose of the plane up, then shut off the power. The plane began to shudder. Suddenly, it flipped upside down and started screaming earthward, spinning violently. I turned loose of the controls and got ready to meet my Maker. Then, just as suddenly as it all began, the plane stopped spinning and leveled out.

"Now, did you see how I thrust the stick forward and kicked in the right rudder?" Captain Tope asked as if it were perfectly obvious.

"No, sir, I didn't," I tried to sound calm, but to me, my voice sounded high and strained.

"Well, let's do it again so you can get a handle on it."

Believe me, flight training was not dull. Those first night flights were hair-raising. On my first night flight the instructor landed the plane then told me to try it. I was still looking for the runway when I flew right onto it. Navy planes don't have landing lights that shine down on the runway. We were training to fly as we would later, off of an aircraft carrier. The Navy doesn't want to light up a carrier at night to show the enemy where to drop his bombs.

I experienced more freedom than I ever had, because now I had more money and more opportunities to spend it. Most nights I went with my buddies to the night clubs around Pensacola. We felt important and invulnerable as we told hair-tingling tales of near catastrophes.

However, my exciting world came crumbling down when my roommate died in a crash. I walked back to our room after I found out. It seemed so quiet now. I stared at his bed. There seemed to be something in the back of my throat that wouldn't go down. I swallowed convulsively. Just the night before we had gone out drinking together, but now he was gone.

Death filled my thoughts. I kept wondering what would happen to me if I got killed. *I think I would go to heaven,* I told myself. *I'm a good guy. God would want to have me around.* Our invulnerability was cracked as training continued. Three students a week were killed. Death became a companion to the pilots, but we tried to drown it every night at the clubs.

We moved to Barin Field for formation training after a number of solo flights. This was even more challenging. We flew very close formations where the chances of hitting the plane next to you was always a fear. Our instructor flew some distance from the six-plane formation and gave directions over the radio.

"Turn to 280, descend to 8,000 feet. Number six, you take the lead. Shift into a V formation."

One of the instructors was infamous for screaming at the students over the radio. I couldn't blame him because we were greenhorns. Some of the other instructors decided to teach him a lesson. "Screaming Meanie" briefed six students one day on where to rendezvous with him. When we started for our planes, six instructors intercepted us. "Go back to the barracks. We'll fly today." They grinned at our shocked expressions.

At the rendezvous point, they met the unsuspecting instructor who began giving directions. "Head out on 150 degrees, shift lead to number four." The six instructors began to do the opposite of everything he said and engaged in all kinds of crazy acrobatics. He started screaming wildly at them and finally commanded them all to land! He called the tower and shouted, "Clear the field! This is an emergency!"

The instructors landed on separate runways going all different directions. "Screaming Meanie" almost had a heart attack! His words became unrecognizable bellows and rants. All this was recorded on tape and we played it over and over, laughing till we cried.

I tried to remember everything and was proud of my ability to fly well. However, I soon found that flying was not the only way you could die.

6

Not an accident

One weekend I drove home to Birmingham to have a little fun with some of my old high school and college buddies. We drank a lot and spent time with some equally wild girls. Our favorite haunts were the roadhouses on Old Highway 280. We kept the jukebox blaring our favorite songs and danced till the early hours. We all had tales about what was happening in our lives. Generally, we just raised Cain.

Late Sunday night I drove by myself back to Pensacola. The late nights had taken their toll and I began to get sleepy. I tried everything to stay awake. I drank Coca-Colas till my eyes were swimming. I held my head out the window like a dog, hoping the cool air would revive me. I tried shutting one eye. Then I tried shutting the other eye. Then I tried shutting both eyes.

Somewhere near the Florida border, the highway curved, but I went straight. My old Studebaker went speeding at sixty mph from smooth pavement onto a rutted-out, washboard road. The quiet swish of the wind changed to a hailstorm as the rocks and gravel pounded the bottom of my car. My head hit the roof, bringing me to full heart-lurching consciousness. The car nearly shook to pieces as I struggled to gain control.

My heart was in my throat and pounding so hard I thought it would jump out of my shirt. Slamming on the brakes, I swung the car around and stopped in a ditch. The dust billowed over the car, and I was submerged in a brown cloud.

The hot engine was ticking under the hood, but

everything else around was very quiet. I couldn't believe I had run off the paved road onto a dirt road.

The countryside night was dark as pitch. As the dust began to settle, I looked up and saw my headlights shining on something large and white right in front of my car. It was a big sign nailed on a tree. What it said shocked me more than my near-fatal accident. I would remember the words on that sign all my life!

In large black letters was written:

"The wages of sin is death."

I thought, *Good grief! I don't believe this is an accident. I think God let me go to sleep and stop right in front of this sign. He's trying to tell me something. I know what He wants. He's telling me 'Shape up or else!' I 've got to change my ways.*

I felt like that was a "star" from God sent to get my attention. Just like the Wise Men who were guided by a special star to the place where Jesus was born, I had several "stars" that guided my life. This was the first.

7

It's not my fault

The only way I knew how to reform was to start going to church. So the next day, when I finished flying, I drove into town and looked around until I found a Presbyterian church. I was seeking spiritual help, but didn't know how to ask for it. I walked into the church office and found a lady sitting at a desk.

"May I help you?" she asked with a big smile.

"I want to get active in church," I said, for that was the only way I knew how to reform.

Apparently she didn't know any more than I did because she asked, "Can you sing in the choir?"

"No ma'am, I can't carry a tune in a bucket."

"Can you teach Sunday school?" was her next question.

"No, ma'am."

"What can you do?"

"Well, I used to be a Boy Scout."

She smiled flatly, "We don't have a Boy Scout troop."

That was that, and all she could offer. I smiled back at her, turned around and walked out, disappointed. That was my only interchange with the church since high school. I did start attending church, but didn't get much help with my behavior. After one service I thought, *I can change my way of living. It's just a matter of making up my mind.*

I went back to the Officer Quarters firmly resolved to do better. Later that afternoon, my roommate walked in. "Come on. We've got dates and we're going over to the Officers' Club and see what develops," he smiled wolfishly.

"I'm not going." I knew we would drink too much

and that would lead me back into what I was trying to get out of.

"What?" he exclaimed, surprise written all over his face. "Are you sick?" he probed.

"No," I tried to look nonchalant.

"Have you gotten religion?" he asked. There had been another accident that week and many men would "get religious" after close calls.

"No," I said, not letting him in on how close he was to the truth.

"Well, okay," he shrugged and went out to have fun, leaving me sitting alone in our bare little room.

My good resolutions lasted about a week. The first real temptation that came along grabbed me and sucked me back in. Again I thought, *Why can't I change? It must be these other guys in this program who are pulling me down. I'm a good person, but they aren't. They're my problem! I need to change friends.*

The next day I approached my flight instructor. "Captain Tope," I said, "I want to speed up the flight program and fly three flights per day instead of two."

He didn't know what my motives were, but agreed to my plan. In the phase of training I was in, the pilots went through individually. If I could finish the first phase before my buddies, I would be sent on to the second phase where I'd be with another group of (hopefully) better guys.

It was hard work, but I advanced to the next level early and was thrown in with a new group of guys. But, to my astonishment, these new friends were just as bad as the old ones. They influenced me in the wrong way, too. I just wound up in the same bars with the same girls. I thought, *these guys are no good either. This program is full of people like this.*

One night while sitting in a bar with a group of Navy men and the girls, I started wondering why I went to these places. I sat on a bar stool sipping a drink and finally figured out why I fell for every temptation. It was as if a light bulb came on in my head. *The reason I end up here is because I like to go out with the fellows and have fun. I enjoy it. I'm no different from all the other guys. It's just like in high school, "Barker, one of the boys."*

Now that I knew what my problem was, I wondered how I could change what I liked to do? Maybe I could convince myself I didn't like girls.

Eventually, I concluded there was no way to change what I liked to do, even though I knew it was wrong. The "power of positive thinking" didn't work for me. I knew I couldn't quit until I stopped enjoying those bad things. So, I decided to quit worrying about it and just have fun. The next year of flight training, I fulfilled that goal easily.

Before I went for advanced training at Corpus Christi, Texas, I remembered that beautiful girl my friend dated at Auburn, Barbara Brown. I wrote her and asked for a date the following weekend. She answered and agreed to go out with me. I thought about her as I drove the long 300 miles to Birmingham. She was different from the "bar girls" I had been with these last years. She was the kind of girl I wanted to marry.

I took her out Old Highway 280 to "Milgens," my favorite roadhouse, where we danced to the jukebox. She was training to be a ballerina and danced gracefully. I couldn't take my eyes off her. I was lost in the most beautiful blue eyes I had ever seen. While we were dancing, I told her, "You know, I love you and you are the girl I want to marry."

She smiled and said, "You've had too much to drink and don't know what you're saying."

I took her by the shoulders and looked into her eyes, "I know what I'm saying, and I'm very serious."

She looked at me thoughtfully and said, "I'm training to be a professional ballet dancer. I'd have to think a long time before I decided to give that up or before I told anyone I loved him."

I wasn't put off by her answer. I felt I could win her if I tried, and I intended on trying hard. I hated leaving her and going back to base.

The next week I was thrilled when I received a letter with her distinctive handwriting on the envelope. I ripped it open and read her words that gave me new hope. She said she did love me and liked the idea of marriage. I immediately wrote her back to finish college first, then we would move in that direction.

That began a sweet, long-distance relationship. Whenever we could, which was not often, we would get together. I never could get enough of being with her and always hated saying goodbye. I was never sure of when I would get to see her again. My training flights were getting more and more difficult and carrier takeoff and landing training was on the horizon. At this point in my basic training, we were flying propeller trainers. In advanced training we progressed to fighter jets.

8

Anything for true love

At the conclusion of my training, I was assigned to a fighter jet squadron on the west coast. I drove my car to San Diego and checked in at my new squadron, VFP 61, at Miramar Naval Air Station. It was a fighter-photo squadron. Our job was to do photo reconnaissance which involved mapping enemy territory and on other occasions, taking pictures of the target area with a camera in the nose of the plane while flying at a very low altitude. Other pilots flying attacks could study the photos and identify the landscape and know where to drop their bombs or shoot their rockets.

VFP 61 was a large squadron with about seventy pilots. Every carrier that left the west coast would have three of our planes and four of our pilots, plus a group of men to maintain the aircraft and cameras and to develop the pictures.

Most of the pilots in the squadron were experienced. Lieutenant J. B. Melton began mentoring me in flying. For cross-country, night-flying experience, we would fly to El Paso. During our short stay there, we rented a car and drove across the border to Mexico to purchase bottles of inexpensive whiskey. On the flight back we carried our precious cargo tucked in our flight suits.

One night when we arrived back at San Diego, a heavy fog had set in and we couldn't see anything on the ground. Several things had gone wrong with my plane on that trip. My tip tanks would not transfer fuel to the engine, so I didn't have enough fuel to fly to an alternate field. My radio had gone out, so I couldn't receive instructions for a ground-controlled approach.

J.B. was my wingman and knew my circumstances. Above the fog we could see each other's faces and hand signals by the moonlight. I got on his wing and we let down our landing gear and flaps and eased down into the fog. I had *never* flown on someone's wing *in the clouds,* much less at night!

I made a few stupid errors. The first was that I got on the wrong side of his plane which positioned me inside the turns. When flying this approach at a very slow speed, my plane stayed on the verge of a stall, and I kept scooting out in front of him. The second mistake was that I left my flashing light on and every time it went on in the cloud, it was like a powerful photo flash in my face that blinded me. Somehow we made it down safely and didn't lose the whiskey! I was pretty shook-up and promptly consumed a large quantity of our purchase.

Sometimes, instead of flying to El Paso, we would fly to Las Vegas, go into town to gamble and see the girlie shows, then fly back that night. Training time was pretty exciting.

As part of my cross-country training, I flew my fighter jet to Chicago where Barbara was in school at Northwestern University. It was pretty exciting to fly my fighter jet in and find my beautiful girlfriend waiting for me. That first kiss after the long flight was like a cool drink of water. The smell of my leather flight jacket, mingled with her perfume, was something I thought about all the way back to California.

Once when I was flying up to Chicago to see her, the cockpit heater was out. Since I had to fly at about 40,000 feet to get the low fuel consumption I needed between airports, and since it was winter, the cockpit temperature was about 20 degrees Fahrenheit. To make it worse, the cockpit pressurization was connected to the heating, so I didn't have adequate cockpit pressure. This caused my oxygen mask to pump oxygen into my mouth and nose. I had to exhale by blowing out with all my might. Then, immediately, oxygen was forcefully pumped back into my mouth and nose. Try that for an hour and a half!

Imagine trying to make position reports under such conditions. Every time I opened my mouth to talk, I was blown up like a balloon! When I landed, Barbara took one look at me and said, "Why is your skin so blue?"

Oh well, anything for true love!

9

Catapult terrors

After finishing my training in photography in a F2H Banshee, I was part of a team assigned to go on a nine-month cruise to Asia. The USS Oriskany was an old, straight-deck carrier which made it essential that, upon landing, our tail hook must catch a cable. Otherwise, we would wind up in a nylon barricade, or even worse, we would hit one of the planes parked on the deck and explode. The newer carriers with canted decks allowed a plane to take off again if it missed a cable.

All the pilots had to qualify for carrier takeoffs and landings in the type of plane they were flying. A month before we sailed, we cruised off the California coast to practice. This was done fairly close to shore because the pilots who couldn't make their six carrier landings needed a place to land near the shore.

That first carrier takeoff could easily have been my last since I had forgotten one of the ten things necessary to stay alive. After my plane was shot from the catapult, it dropped toward the water. I thought, *This is it! I'm going to die*. Just before I hit the water, my engine kicked in. I licked the top wave and felt the jet lurch forward. It seemed I had defied death yet again. I came around and landed. I was catapulted off and landed five more times and was qualified.

I would never again forget those ten things. I could repeat them in my sleep years later.

This was my second wake-up call, my second "star" that seemed to point the direction I was supposed to go. I knew God must have something He wanted me to do because there was no reason I should have survived that first catapult.

I knew I had to change my ways. I tried again. Nothing changed. As soon as the qualifying cruise was over, I was back to my old habits.

The Oriskany sailed a month later. When aircraft were to be launched, the reconnaissance planes were always the first off and the first to land back on the carrier. As soon as the carrier turned into the wind, the first plane was to be launched.

On one occasion, I was first up. My plane was positioned on the right hand catapult and my engine was screaming. I saluted the catapult officer and he gave the signal to fire my catapult. They pressed the button and nothing happened! The catapult didn't go off! I looked at him and he looked at me and sweat beaded both our faces in spite of the fifty knot wind.

If I pulled the throttle back and then the catapult went off, I was dead. If I didn't pull it back, the crew couldn't get near the plane to check why the catapult hadn't gone off. Finally, the catapult officer walked in front of the plane and gave me the throttle back signal. In effect he was saying, "If you get killed, I get killed with you."

I throttled back and the catapult crew scrambled all over the area checking the catapult. It appeared they found the problem. So, again, he gave me the signal to rev up my engine. I did, again saluted, and he gave the signal to fire me. They pressed the button, and again nothing happened.

Now we were really sweating! Once more he walked in front and signaled to throttle back. They decided that catapult was broken and moved my plane over to the left catapult. I again revved up the engine and saluted. He gave the signal and this catapult thrust my plane forward. The only problem was that, by now, everyone was very nervous, and they had scaled this catapult's thrust up much stronger than normal for my size airplane. The resulting force was so powerful that it broke the hydraulic line in my seat. As I went off the ship, my seat, which I had jacked up because I'm short, bottomed out on me and I had trouble seeing over the instrument panel. My plane wobbled all over the sky for a few minutes.

"Are you OK?" the carrier radio operator asked.

"I think so," I said. "Just give me a few minutes to get my wits together!" I always thought about Barbara in times like this.

When those types of things happened, I would get religious for a week. I would go to Sunday services on the hanger deck that were conducted by the chaplain. It was after one such episode that I even joined the choir, much to everyone's surprise, since I'm nearly tone deaf. We practiced for several weeks and then the day came when we were to perform.

On the hanger deck there are blowers that make a lot of racket. One was right by us, and I wanted the congregation of about 400 sailors to hear us. Just before we were to sing, I told the choir member sitting next to me to push the button on the wall to cut it off. He got up and pushed the button, but it wasn't the blower switch. He activated the automatic sprinkler! Immediately, dozens of nozzles in the ceiling drenched the congregation. The sprinkler didn't stop until it was empty.

The captain of the ship looked disgusted. He and the commander of the air group were sitting on the front row. They got up and walked out. Everyone else sat there getting soaked. When the water finally stopped, the choir performed and the chaplain preached. It would have been appropriate if he had preached on Noah and the Flood or said, "Now you are all baptized."

Deadly antics

Before I got off active duty, I did two more cruises on aircraft carriers. One was on the Kearsarge, a straight-deck carrier, the other on the Shangrila. It had a canted deck and was significantly easier to land on. A landing signal mirror replaced the LSO (Landing Signal Officer) who used to be stationed on a platform at the left-hand side of the rear deck, directing the pilots with phosphorescent "paddles." This large, concave mirror reflected a beam of light that guided us. As the pilots looked at the mirror, there was a bright light like a small sun in the center and a horizontal row of lights across it. We focused on the beam as we came down to land. If the bright glow was higher than the row of lights, we were coming in too high. If the beam was lower than the row, we were too low. If red lights suddenly flashed, we had to wave off and go around again. Instead of pulling the throttle off when we landed, like we did on the straight-deck carriers, we landed with full power. If our tail hook didn't catch a cable, we took off and came around again. It was hard to override all my previous training to throttle back and retrain my instincts to give full throttle as I came onto the carrier.

These cruises in Asia did not involve combat since the Korean War was over. On my nine-month cruise, we put in at Yokosuka, Japan, and went ashore for a few days. We also flew our planes to Atsugi Air Base and operated out of there.

The Japanese were friendly. We squeezed into the subways that were packed with more people than I had ever seen in one place. We toured various cities whenever we got a break from flying. One of our favorite sites was Mount Fuji. It was an amazing sight! Tokyo was huge, but we always managed to find someone who spoke English to help us get around!

A tragic accident happened on our carrier's return trip. When we neared Okinawa, I and my wingman were assigned to map the Air Force airfield there. We flew back and forth over the field, straight and level, mapping it. Meanwhile, some Air Force fighters began harassing us. They made passes at us, turned loops and made our work difficult.

When we finished mapping I said to my wingman, "Let's go get those guys!" If I could go back now and change the past, I would have flown straight back to our carrier. Who would have thought harmless pranks would cause such calamity?

I saw several Air Force jets taking off, and we dove down toward them. About the time they got airborne, we whipped under and zipped right out in front of them. "That'll teach those Air Force boys not to mess with the Navy!"

Obviously, such antics were against the rules, but we often engaged in them. We pulled up to about 10,000 feet and headed back to the carrier not expecting a chase. However, they did come after us. They tried to get on our tail.

"Here they come," I said to my wingman. "Get ready to break right. Now, break!" As we turned sharply to the right, I heard an explosion. I rolled to the left and there, just off my wing, was what looked like a blazing sun! I thought they had hit my wingman. The two Air Force jets had collided. There was not a piece larger than a dinner plate left. Both pilots were killed instantly.

I was ordered to the Air Force base for a court of inquiry a few days later, but was not disciplined in any way by the military. I couldn't stop thinking about those guys who died because of our pranks. When I closed my eyes at night, I saw that fireball over and over. I wished I could turn back time. God was getting my attention.

Growing up, my mother and father had taught me to kneel by my bed every night and pray. It never occurred to me not to do it. Even on the carrier I knelt by my bunk and prayed like this: "God, bless Mama and Daddy and Sister and the dog. Forgive me for doing all these bad things, and help me to be different." My prayers had been no more than a rabbit's foot a kid carries for good luck.

One night I rattled off my prayer and had a strange feeling that God was listening. I didn't hear anything or see anything, but felt that He was saying, "Do you really want to be different? Or are you just talking?"

It was a solemn moment. If I said "yes," I believed He would do something inside me that would really change me. And I really didn't want to change. I didn't want to be different. I wondered, *What is it going to cost in my lifestyle?*

Then a shocking thought occurred to me. *What are you doing? You are resisting God!! That's dumb! All He would have to do is snap His fingers and that catapult would throw your jet right in the ocean. Whatever changes He wants to make in your life, wouldn't that be the best thing? Can't I trust Him for what He wants with my life? Can I even trust myself with my life? Didn't He love me and send His Son to die for me?*

I prayed, "God, it is foolish to resist you. I really do want your will done in my life, whatever it is."

My next thought was, *when I say that, I am planning to do*

something next weekend that I know He doesn't approve of. How can I be sincere? That's right! I can't be sincere and still be planning on going through with something I know He doesn't want me to do.

Not to go through with my plan would involve a lot of flack from my squadron buddies. I really cared about the peer pressure. I prayed, "All right, God, I won't do what I was planning next weekend, but You've got to get me out of it. I really care what my buddies think."

I got up from my knees and knew God had heard me. I took steps to extricate myself from the weekend plans. I was conscious of God working behind the scenes making it not quite as tough as I thought it would be.

That became a pattern. Something would get on my mind to drag me down, so I would ask the Lord to help me by arranging circumstances that would allow me to overcome the temptation. Six months later I had made some sizable moral changes.

Then I got the feeling God wanted me to go to seminary and be a minister. I said, "Wait a minute! You've got the wrong guy, Lord. I'm an Auburn engineer!"

But I couldn't shake the feeling that God wanted me to be a minister. I wrote my mother that when I finished my tour of duty, I planned on going to seminary. She was shocked and delighted. My sister didn't believe it. When Mother read my letter to her she said, "What? Read that again!"

Hours of boredom with moments of terror

When my carrier returned to San Diego, California, I continued going to my VFP 61 Squadron parties. But instead of joining in the drinking of alcohol I just had a soft drink. Our squadron commander, who had a drinking problem, began to pick up on this.

"What are you drinking?" he asked.

I could see the despair in his eyes but also that he hoped that if I didn't drink booze, maybe he too could get along without it.

"A Coke," I answered.

"Get me one. I don't really want to drink, but I don't want the other pilots to think I'm not one of them." I was happy my example was helping him.

The next weekend several pilots were going to fly to Pensacola to have dates with our girlfriends. From there I planned to rent a car and drive to Birmingham to see Barbara.

I had just been checked out in a F9F-8 Cougar which was a new plane in our squadron. The other two pilots were well experienced in it. We flew to El Paso where we refueled. One of the experienced pilots said, "We've got to land again at Navy Dallas for fuel. Since that's a fairly short hop and we're running late, just burn off your internal tanks, not the wing tanks. That way the refueling won't take so long."

I thought, *Boy, he's really using his brain*. I did what he recommended.

The pilot who had advised me to use the internal tanks began thinking about the situation and decided the plane might be unstable with low internal fuel and full wing tanks. He decided to use his wing tanks but forgot to advise me to do the same.

When we neared Navy Dallas, we were told that a plane had just crashed on the 10,000 foot runway and we should use a short 5,000 foot runway.

It was night when we flew over the field, and we were in a right echelon formation. The experienced pilot peeled to the left first. I was second and the other pilot, third. As we came around the field in a left-hand turn, we had to slow down to prepare for landing. I had to get some distance between the front plane and mine. As I slowed my plane to get below 150 knots, the jet became unstable because of the full wing tanks.

The first pilot made a perfect landing, and I came in right behind him but too fast. I slammed on my brakes with my whole weight. My right tire blew out and my plane began swinging off the runway. Trying to stay on the runway, I was stomping hard on the brakes when the other tire blew. From that point on, I had no control of the plane.

The plane in front of me was slowing down even more.

"LOOK OUT! HERE I COME!" I was shouting in my mike. All I could see was his tailpipe blazing fire right in front of me. I felt like I was tied to a bomb!

The tower operator was going crazy as he watched me closing fast on the front plane. He kept shouting, "Turn off! Turn off onto the taxi strip!"

Sparks were flying from the rims of my wheels on the concrete!

"Turn! Turn!" I screamed.

Just before I would have rammed him, the pilot saw me barreling down on him and finally turned. I whizzed past him like a rocket. My jet flew off the end of the runway. There was something reflecting ahead of me. I realized with dread it was a lake. Now I wouldn't burn to death, but I would drown.

It had been raining for a week and the ground was very soft. My plane ran into the mud and jerked to a stop, sinking up to the fuselage. Dad's prayers were answered again. The Lord was looking after me.

Someone has said flying is "hours and hours of utter boredom interspersed with moments of stark terror." That is the sheer truth! I was shaking like a leaf when I climbed out of the plane.

The ground crew came out with a crane, lifted my plane up, changed the tires and shortly we were again on our way to Pensacola.

When I got to see Barbara, I knew she was certainly worth a little "stark terror."

12

That boy will never be a pastor

I knew I had told God I'd go to seminary, but I had no idea how to go about it. *Where are seminaries anyway?* I was supposed to go on another cruise before too long and thought, *I need to figure out what to do. I'd better go home to Birmingham and ask my pastor for advice.*

I had two weeks leave due, so I packed up my car and drove from California to Birmingham. It was good to be home, sleep in my own bed and eat Mother's cooking. But my mind couldn't rest until I got my plans settled. The second day home, I drove down to my old church fully intending to talk to the pastor. I parked the car and sat there looking at the beautiful, old, gray stone church. The longer I sat, the more I panicked. I couldn't make myself get out of the car and go in. I drove away quickly.

Every day for the next week, I drove back to the church and sat in my car staring at it. I just couldn't make myself go in. I feared that once I told the pastor I was considering seminary, I'd actually have to go through with it. So many doubts plagued me. I was afraid to take that first step.

The days went by quickly until only two days were left before I had to leave for California. On my last day I was playing golf at Birmingham Country Club. As I was getting ready to tee off on the sixteenth hole I thought, *I don't know why I can't go down to the church and talk to my pastor. It's some mental block. If I could only meet the pastor here on the golf course, I could tell him.*

I felt safe because I remembered once hearing the pastor say something about his annual golf game. I relaxed because I knew he wouldn't be on the course today. I drove my ball hard down the fairway, but it sliced and hit a tree. I shuffled around in the grass looking for my ball. When I found it, I looked up right into my pastor's face. At first I thought he was a figment of my imagination. Then I realized God must have timed this "chance" meeting.

Before I could change my mind I said, "Dr. Mathis, I need to talk to you."

"When you finish playing come on down to the church. I'll be waiting," he said.

I didn't even shower but went straight to the church and told him I was considering going to seminary. He seemed really pleased.

"I would advise you to apply to Columbia Seminary in Atlanta. That's where I went, and it's a good one." Turning from his desk he took several books off the overstuffed bookcase. "I'd like for you to begin reading some books that will prepare you."

"I'm sure I need to read these. No one ever went into the ministry knowing less about it. But first, I think I need to make some changes in my life." I wanted to try out my theory on him about being like a Catholic chaplain I had met.

"What kind of changes?" he asked with eyebrows raised.

"Oh," I said sheepishly, "I take an occasional drink."

"That will have to stop!" he said emphatically.

Shoot! The drinking Catholic chaplain can't be my example. As far as Dr. Mathis was concerned, a Presbyterian pastor shouldn't drink. I'd have to quit.

Years later I found out that after I left his office, he walked out shaking his head and told Mrs. Cox, his secretary, "That boy will never make a pastor."

13

Shot in the dark

After my later two cruises, I had about 700 hours of jet flight time, and with flight training included, I had fulfilled my required four years of active duty. In the meantime, I had been promoted from Ensign to Lieutenant Junior Grade. I received my discharge papers and was ready to get on with life.

My preacher, Dr. Mathis, set up an interview for me with the Presbytery. To go to seminary I had to be officially accepted as a candidate for the ministry. I stood up in front of all those distinguished, old men feeling like it was easier to be shot from a catapult than stand up there. I had to tell them why I thought God had called me to be a minister.

After listening to me a white-haired gentleman in the back stood up and asked, "Young man, are you saved?"

What? I had no idea what he was talking about. No one had ever asked me that before. But here I was before a hundred people including my mom and dad.

"Yes, sir," I said, hoping that was the right answer.

He asked, "How do you know?"

I made a shot in the dark. I said, "Jesus tells us." This was always the answer in Sunday school for any question.

"That's right," he nodded his approval and sat down.

Off I went to seminary, not sure of what "saved" meant, but hoping to find out.

I went to my pastor's alma mater, Columbia Theological in Atlanta. At first I was very confused. In one of my classes the professor was tearing the Bible apart, and in the next class the professor was trying to put it together. In my heart I asked, is the Bible *true*?

One of my professors taught that when Moses lead the Israelites across the Red Sea it was really only a marshy area. "The waters are shallow. In fact, this phenomenon has been witnessed at other times."

I thought that was plain funny. How could it be so shallow that the Israelites walked across and the Egyptians drowned?

His explanation of God's miraculous provision of manna during the Exodus was also troubling. He said, "Manna probably refers to a sweet, sticky substance produced by a number of insects that suck plants' sap in dry desert areas. The sap falls to the ground and is consumed quickly by ants during the day. During the night, however, it accumulates and can be gathered for food."

Whoa! I thought. *That's a lot of sticky insect sap to feed more than a million people?*

Another professor taught Universalism, the concept that everyone is going to be saved regardless of whether he believes in Jesus. *How did that man get a job teaching in a Christian seminary?* I wondered.

When I raised objections the professor said, "You know the trouble with you, Barker?"

I said, "Which one?"

"When they dig Jesus' body up in Palestine, it's going to destroy your faith," he replied. "It isn't necessary to believe Christ rose from the dead in order to believe in Christ."

"I don't think they will dig Him up," I countered, but he brushed me off.

There were other professors I respected very much. Dr. Manford George Gutzke was one of them. *He has what I want,* I thought. *Whenever he teaches a class, I'm going to take it whether I need it or not.*

One of Dr. Gutzky's classes was on prophecy. I looked at prophecy through my engineering background because I wanted something solid to get my teeth into. He taught that most prophecies were written at least 285 years before Jesus was born. Some were actually given 750 to 1,000 years before His birth.

This is one thing that sets the Bible apart from all other "religious books." Not only does it make these astounding prophecies about Christ, but they were also fulfilled to the last detail. Through Christ's birth, life and death, more than 300 prophecies were fulfilled.

I was particularly interested in the Wise Men, who searched for God's Son. They were led to Jerusalem by a unique star. There, they met Herod who inquired of the Old Testament scholars, the Scribes, where the Messiah was to be born. They said, "Bethlehem," and then quoted Micah 5:2 which predicted in 700 BC that He would be born there. I thought about all the ways God had guided me like the sign, **"The wages of sin is death,"** I read when I drove off the highway. Then there were the near-death experiences I had while flying. I thought of these things as "stars." They guided me to seminary just like the real star had guided the Wise Men to Jesus. I wondered again what God had in store for my life.

14

Oxford and orphans

About a month after I started seminary, my roommate walked in and said, "I'm pastoring a church in Oxford, Alabama, on the weekends. But I graduate this quarter and I'm moving. They won't have a pastor. How about taking it for me?"

"I just got here!" I said, incredulous that he even asked me. "I don't know a thing!"

"They need a pastor," he pleaded.

I had to preach to the church before they invited me to be their pastor, so I prepared a sermon. I asked my roommate and two other students to listen. After I "delivered" it, I asked for comments.

No one looked at me. Silence. Tick, tick, tick the clock by my bed sounded like a church bell.

Finally someone said, "Maybe you'd better not go."

It was my first and only sermon. I worked hard to improve it and made some changes they suggested. Oxford is about halfway between Atlanta and Birmingham, and I drove over early Sunday morning. When I found the little white frame church I thought, *that's what a church should look like*. It had been built before the Civil War.

The congregation, seventeen strong, must have thought my sermon wasn't too bad because they asked me to be their pastor. Actually, I was only a student supply, but I was hired. Now I really was a minister, but still didn't understand the gospel.

This was May of 1957. I pastored the church on weekends for two years. I enjoyed the people, and they encouraged me. I guess I looked pretty young to them, and they thought of me as their son.

During the fall and winter school semesters, I drove over to Oxford on Saturday. I visited the sick then worked on my sermon for Sunday. One of the church members invited me to stay in his home so I didn't have to stay in a motel.

For the Sunday evening service, I didn't preach but led a Bible study. By the time I started back to Atlanta late at night, I was very weary and often nearly went to sleep. Remembering my near crash when I dozed driving back to Pensacola, I forced myself to stay awake.

One weekend a month I flew in the Naval Air Reserves. On that weekend I'd get another student to fill in at the church. I loved flying and it gave me the freedom I still craved. I didn't feel free in seminary. I was just fulfilling an obligation I felt I owed to God.

The church pianist was an older woman who played the piano so slowly it seemed the songs would never end. It drove me crazy. I said, "Mrs. Jones, we need to speed up the singing a bit."

"Oh, Mr. Barker, I'm afraid I will get ahead of them if I play any faster," she said.

I tried to be patient. "Let's give it a try," I said. "I'll watch and if they can sing faster, I'll wipe my forehead with my handkerchief."

She agreed to watch me and speed up if I wiped my forehead.

Sunday, she played "Rock of Ages" in her same funeral tempo. I took out my handkerchief and wiped my forehead. She increased the tempo a tiny bit. I had to keep my handkerchief going throughout the whole hymn. She kept watching me with raised brows as if to say, "Are you sure?"

Driving over to Oxford for my "pastoring," I thought about how to get the church growing. There were no families with children. We needed young families if the church was to survive. At the end of my first year, I suggested that we start a Sunday school for children.

"Mr. Barker, we don't have space for Sunday school," an older man in the group reminded me.

"Why don't we use the parsonage for our classes?" I asked.

"We rent that out and use the money to pay you."

"Why not pay me out of the contributions?" I asked.

"We use those to support the Presbytery and we are the highest contributors to it!" was their proud response.

I couldn't believe this little country church sent all their money to the Presbytery. I tried to reason with them, "The money would be better used to get this church growing by having a Sunday school where young couples could bring their children." They finally agreed and we grew to sixty-two members in my second year there.

As if I didn't have enough to do my first year in school, a classmate took me to the orphanage across the street from the seminary. He was leading a worship service for the children there on Wednesday nights. Because he was graduating, he asked if I would take over.

I felt compassion for all those kids who had no mom or dad. I thought about my parents. They had loved me so much and prayed for me every day. I wanted to help those kids who didn't know the kind of love that I had taken for granted.

There were about 150 children in the service from ages five to seventeen. With such a wide age group, it would be a challenge to teach in a way that all of them could understand. Maybe if I told Bible stories and made an application, everyone would learn something. With this plan in mind, I agreed to take over for him.

I ate supper with a different cottage group each week before the large meeting. The time with the kids was always fun. It was a relief from the tedium of reading and studying for my classes. Learning to tell the stories so they "come alive" and became applicable to their lives gave me experience that I have used through the years. I grew to love the children and their house parents as I taught them during the next two years I was in seminary.

I'm sure people who knew me would say that I was different because I was in seminary and wasn't going out drinking every night, but I still felt like the same old person. I wondered if I would ever really change.

15

The finger in my face

During that first year in seminary, one of my squadron buddies from Miramar was getting married in Athens, Georgia. He wanted me to be in the wedding. It was a military wedding and I wore my old uniform. After the ceremony there was a reception at the country club. I rode with the naval officers who were also in the wedding. Before leaving the church parking lot, the driver opened the trunk of his car and took out a fifth of whiskey. Laughing, he took a swig and passed the bottle to his right. It was just like old times, everyone tipping it back and passing it along.

What am I going to do when it gets to me? I remembered my pastor and how he looked down on drinking. *Oh, well, no one knows I'm a minister, and I don't want to be different.* When it was handed to me, I took a swig.

At the reception there was an open bar and also a punch bowl. I got some punch and caught up on news from my Navy friends. Later that evening one gentleman stumbled near me; he was drunk. I heard his wife plead with him, "Please, John, don't drink any more. You know what happens when you drink too much."

John turned to me. I stood rigid with horror seeing him point his stubby finger at me. "The preacher was drinking!" he fairly bellowed. In my mind everyone grew quiet and looked at me.

He had seen me accept the bottle in the parking lot! My taking a swig had not gone unnoticed! I wished I could disappear. I had wanted to fit in, but now I really stood out.

That was the last drink I ever had. I didn't ever want to be the excuse for someone else to get drunk again. I was miserable.

I drove to Birmingham to see Barbara who was teaching at Mountain Brook Junior High. She asked me that weekend when we would be getting married. Now more than ever, I felt like a blind man trying to find my way.

"I love you very much, Barbara, but I can't get married until I figure out what I'm doing. I'm not sure about being a minister. Now is just not the time."

We had been dating five years and she was tired of waiting for me to make a commitment. I didn't want to break off our relationship, but she was angry and hurt that I kept putting her off.

I drove back to Atlanta feeling more lonely than I had ever felt. I knew she wouldn't wait forever. *What if I lose her?* replayed through my mind over and over. I was consumed with school and plagued with my own questions about what I was doing. I couldn't be distracted with marriage.

After pastoring the Church in Oxford for a year I started wondering *What is a Christian? Am I a Christian? How can I be sure I'm a Christian?* I didn't know. But who could I ask? I was the preacher! I thought, *Whatever it is, it's got to be in the Bible. I'm going to figure it out.*

I sat long hours in the library and poured over the Bible trying to understand it. The phrase, "Whoever believes in Jesus Christ has eternal life," jumped off the page. Then I read that God loved us so much He sent Jesus. If we believe in Him, He gives us eternal life.

That's it! I nearly shouted in the quiet library. I looked around and saw fellows quietly reading their books and scribbling notes. *Maybe they already knew this. I had better keep quiet.*

Then I thought, *But what does it mean to believe in Him? I think I believe.* I had been reading for so long I was getting tired, but felt like I had stumbled onto something huge. I leaned back in my chair. *Does it mean to believe that He is who He claimed to be: the Son of God who became man? And to believe that He died for my sin and rose from the grave? If that's what it means, I believe. But, I'm not sure that's all it means to believe.* I simply couldn't figure it all out.

As I look back, I could see all the ways God was leading me to Himself. I began to think of His guidance as stars. Not a real one like the Wise Men saw, but a spiritual equivalent. The first "star" God used was circumstances. The car lights pointing in the night to the sign that read **"The wages of sin is death"** and the fighter jet accidents were circumstances God used to get my attention and woo me to Him.

My next guiding "star" was a man. Joe Lee, an Air Force chaplain, was in some of my classes. He was taking postgraduate work at the seminary, and we became friends. Since I was in the Naval Air Reserves, he went flying with me.

One day he asked me, "Frank, my brother lives in Dallas and is sick. Would you fly me out there?"

I was glad for the opportunity because I felt like I could ask him all my questions.

The plane I flew was an AD6. It was a big, single-engine, propeller plane used to give close air support in combat. It had two side-by-side seats in the cockpit which would make it easy to have a long talk with Joe.

I told the ground crew to fill the extra fuel tank attached to the belly of the plane. That tank can get water from condensation, so it's necessary to drain it before filling. The plane sits at an angle when parked and it must be jacked up before draining the tank or some water will remain. Apparently the attendant didn't know that.

Joe and I took off. I switched to the belly tank to use its fuel first. When it got about time for it to run dry, I told Joe, "Watch the fuel pressure gauge. When you see it drop, tell me, so I can switch tanks."

Before the gauge indicated the gas was low, the engine suddenly started coughing and sputtering and barely running. I flipped the switch to the other tanks expecting it to catch back up. It didn't! Water had shot right into the engine!

I looked down and we were right over Columbus Air Force Base in Columbus, Mississippi.

"Mayday! Mayday!" I yelled into the mike. We plunged down. The engine was coughing and barely sputtering and I struggled to keep the plane level. With much difficulty, I made an emergency landing.

Joe was shaking when he climbed out of the plane. "That was a close one, Frank. I don't think I can go up again. I'll just catch the bus on to Dallas."

"I don't blame you a bit," I said, but I was disappointed that I didn't get to ask him those questions.

The ground crew at Columbus worked on the plane several hours and got it ready to fly. I assured myself that I would have a little talk with that attendant when I got back to Dobbins.

Joe did fly with me again. The next time I brought up the subject before anything else went wrong.

"Joe, what does it mean to believe in Jesus Christ?"

He didn't act surprised or look at me like I was stupid. He reassured me, "Frank, that's something many people struggle with. I have a little booklet that I give to people to help them understand. In fact, it is called 'What Does It Mean to Believe?'"

I tucked it in my pocket and could hardly wait to read it.

That afternoon when I got back to my room, I pulled it out. The booklet said being a Christian is not just believing certain things about Jesus. It's a personal trust in Him: trusting in who He is and what He did for us.

Joe had given me another little book by the same author that explained what it means to trust in Jesus.

Suppose three men died and approached the gate of heaven. God asked each man, "Why should I let you into my heaven?"

The first man said, "I tried to live a good life. I tried to keep your commandments. You ought to let me in."

God said, "In other words you think you've been good enough. If you have been good enough to get to heaven, I didn't need to send my Son to die. I require perfection. Only my Son lived a perfect life."

The first man was not admitted.

The second man approached the gate and said, "I should be allowed into heaven for two reasons. First, I believe in Jesus Christ as my Savior. Second, I was pretty good."

God said, "You contradicted yourself."

"How?" asked the man.

"You said you believed in My Son as your Savior, which is to say you are trusting in Him to save you. That's what it means to believe in My Son. But then you said, 'I was pretty good.' You have one foot on My Son and one foot on your own record. My Son is solid rock. Your record is quicksand. You can't trust in yourself. That's what you need saving from. You need all your faith in Him and none in yourself."

This man was not admitted.

The third man approached the gate and told God, "You shouldn't accept me for what I have done because I am a sinner like everyone else. But I understand that You sent Your Son to die for my sins. I put my whole trust in Him to save me."

God asked, "You mean your only hope is My Son? Is that all you have to offer?"

"Yes, Sir."

"That is faith in My Son. COME ON IN."

When I read that, my reaction was, *That's wrong. It's too easy. That would be a gift. God's not going to give this thing away. You've got to earn it.*

I picked up my Bible and started reading to prove this wrong. Suddenly, I came to that verse I had seen on the sign, "The wages of sin is death." I had never seen what the last half of that verse said, "the gift of God is eternal life through Jesus Christ our Lord."

Good grief! IT IS A GIFT!

The Bible also said God saves you because of His great grace. It is His gift which no one deserves. You can't do anything to earn it or you might brag.

I realized I was the second man at the gate. I had come to seminary out of a dual motive. One, I believed God wanted me to. Two, I had been so bad that if I was going to get to heaven, I was going to have to be a preacher.

I thought if I were a better person, God would accept me. I realized that no matter how much I improved, I still didn't deserve God's forgiveness. Seminary and being good weren't going to get me to heaven. No matter how much I improved, I still wasn't perfect. Only Jesus lived a perfect life. That qualified Him to pay for my sin. I told God I wanted Him to save me, and I now trusted in Jesus' death alone to make me right with Him.

The Lord didn't suddenly appear to me. I didn't have any warm feelings. But I felt like I had found the missing piece of the puzzle. I knew I couldn't change myself. Only God could change me from the inside out.

My life began to change dramatically when I met those two conditions of repentance and faith. I hadn't understood what faith was. I thought it was just believing something was true. I had missed the "trust" part of faith.

Immediately I became more sensitive to sin. I determined to stop thinking impure thoughts about women. One day when I was at the student center getting my mail, I ran into a former Air Force pilot whose box was next to mine. As I reached for my mail, he reached for his and pulled out the new edition of Playboy.

"Man, I'm trying to crawl out of that pit. I can't believe you're jumping in head first!"

He replied, "Oh, it's OK. I can handle it."

He lasted another year longer before dropping out of seminary.

16

Cross in the fog

During my time at Miramar I was assigned to fly with the Blue Angels. I took movies of their amazing aerobatics with the camera in the nose of my jet. We did the shots from a Navy airfield in the desert east of San Diego. I flew with them daily for several weeks. Those movies later comprised the core of a television program of their performances.

One weekend I flew back to Miramar to see my friends. It was night-time and the weather was bad. After making a successful, ground-controlled approach under difficult conditions, I landed. As I turned off the runway onto the taxi strip, the tower asked, "Do you want the 'Follow Me' truck?" This was a small truck that they would send to lead you in. Naval air stations are dimly lighted like aircraft carriers, and we don't have headlights on our planes.

I thought, *I've been flying with the Blue Angels. I don't need any kiddie car to guide me.* So I said, "No thanks. This is my home base. I know the way."

I taxied along the strip until I came to two blue lights close together. That meant an intersection. I turned right and kept close to what I thought was that taxiway's left-hand row of lights. Since nothing was ever parked in the taxiway, I didn't bother to look ahead or to my right as I clipped along to my squadron's parking area.

Suddenly, something seemed to prompt me to look ahead. There, slightly to my right, I saw a glowing cross shining in the fog. Crossed wands is the signal for emergency stop. I screeched to a halt. The enlisted man who had been notified to guide my plane to its parking area was standing in front of me on the tarmac. He took the wand off of his flashlight and shined it around. About ten yards in front of me was a parked plane. If he hadn't stopped me, I would have hit it and blown him up along with the whole end of the field.

What I had thought was the left-hand row of lights had actually been the right-hand row. The only reason I hadn't hit a plane already was that the squadron that normally parked its planes in the area where I was taxiing had moved out to a carrier that weekend!

The enlisted man had no way to communicate with the tower or with me. All he could do was bravely hold up his crossed wands and hope that I would see them. I knew he would have diligently stayed there until I collided with my squadron's plane and been blown up with me.

Remembering that brave man who saved my life reinforced what another Man, Christ Jesus, had done when I was headed for destruction. I am eternally grateful for both.

17

The gift

I wondered why no one had told me that salvation was a gift. Then I thought, *Isn't it strange that Martin Luther didn't know that.* The reason I thought about Luther was that I had just read his commentary on Galations for a course I was taking. If Luther had known that salvation is a gift, he would have brought it out in the book! I wanted to see how he had missed it, so I pulled the commentary off the shelf and reread it. To my amazement, it was on every page!

I thought, *I must have been blind when I read this book!* It dawned on me that God has to open a person's spiritual eyes to understand the Scripture. I had been trying to do it on my own. Why God used that tract instead of Luther's commentary is a mystery.

Another change God made in my life concerned my tithing. I had been taught to tithe as a child. When I graduated from college and went into the service, I had them take a tenth of my pay and send it to my home church. I had even tithed my earnings from gambling.

Now that I understood salvation was a gift, I wanted to express my gratitude for God's amazing grace; but I didn't know how. The idea occurred to me to express my gratitude by increasing the percent I tithed each year. I started trying to do it, and it wasn't hard. I was on the G.I. Bill which paid my tuition. Pastoring the church on the weekends brought in $100 a month, and being in the Naval Air Reserve gave me enough money to raise the percentage some more.

Also, I became concerned about other people knowing

that salvation was a gift of God. I thought, *Do my parents know about this?* The next time I went home, I blurted out my question during supper, "Mother and Dad, do you both understand that salvation is a gift, that you don't earn it or deserve it?"

"Yes," they said with big smiles on their faces.

"Why didn't you tell me?" I quizzed.

"We did, Son. But it didn't soak in. God had to open your eyes, and we are so thankful that He has."

"Oh," I said. "All right. Thank you."

What about my sister? She was my next concern. Did she know? Next day I drove over to her house and asked, "Minnie Lee, do you understand that salvation is a gift?"

"No, Frank. I don't know that." She accepted Christ with me that day.

My next thought was, *I've got to tell Barbara.* We had broken up, and she had moved to the west coast. I wrote her a letter and explained the gospel to her. Unknown to me, Barbara had been so depressed after we had broken up that she took an overdose of aspirin to try to kill herself. Her sister Anita had explained the gospel to her, and she had prayed to receive Christ.

Charlie was a handyman who lived in a servant's house behind Mother and Dad's home. He worked for our family and other neighbors. We considered him as part of our family.

Driving home from seminary one weekend I thought, *I ought to talk to Charlie about Christ.* When I pulled into our driveway, a light was on in Charlie's house. Before going in to see my parents, I walked up to Charlie's and knocked on the door.

He opened the door and a wide smile lit up his weathered face. "Hello, Mr. Frank."

"Hello, Charlie. Can I come in a minute?"

"I'm so glad to see you home," Charlie said and ushered me in.

"It's good to be home," I said. We talked a few minutes, and then I said, "Charlie, something has been on my heart. Do you know for sure that when you die you will go to heaven?"

"Well, I think I will," he said rubbing his chin and furrowing his brow like my question worried him.

"Why do you think that?"

"Well, Mr. Frank, I haven't done anything real bad," he said and looked at me as if he wanted me to confirm it.

"Charlie, the Bible says the wages of our sin is death. That's talking about hell."

"Now, if the wages of sin is death," Charlie answered, "I am in trouble. But I don't sin a whole lot." A glimmer of hope shown in his eyes.

I knew a particular sin of Charlie's. On occasion I had bailed him out of jail when he was arrested for drunkenness. I said, "Let me read you a verse of Scripture, Charlie." I turned to First Corinthians 6 and read the verse that says drunkards shall not inherit the kingdom of God.

Charlie's face was solemn.

"Now, Charlie, what are we going to do about this?"

"I'll just have to try harder to be better and ask God to forgive me."

"When you were in jail for breaking the law, if you had told the judge you were going to try to be better and that you wanted him to forgive you, would he have forgiven you?"

"No," he said shaking his head and looking at the floor.

"How did you get out of jail?"

"Mr. Frank, you came and paid my fine."

"Suppose God were to allow someone to pay your fine for breaking His law. The only problem is, it wouldn't be $25.00 because the penalty for breaking His law is death. Do you know someone who would die in your place? God would forgive you on that basis."

A mental struggle wrinkled Charlie's brow as he thought it over. He shook his head and said, "Mr. Frank, I have a lot of friends, but I don't believe I have a single friend who would die for me."

"But Charlie, you do. Jesus Christ so loved you, Charlie, that He died and paid your fine, just like I used to pay your fine."

Tears filled Charlie's eyes and rolled down his black face. He said, "Mr. Frank, that's good news."

"Would you like to kneel over here by the sofa and ask God to forgive your sins, Charlie?"

"Yes, Sir, I shore would," he said and jumped out of his chair and beat me to the sofa.

"Would you like for me to lead you in a prayer to God?" I asked. I prayed, and he repeated my words asking God to forgive his sins and Jesus Christ to come into his heart and be his Savior.

When we stood up, Charlie could hardly contain his joy. He nearly shook my hand off and thanked me again and again for telling him about the Lord.

When I saw anyone come to Christ or take significant steps in growing spiritually, my own heart would fill with joy. One night after sharing the gospel with a couple, I thought, *I had rather do this than anything else in the world! The excitement of flying jets doesn't hold a candle to the excitement of seeing someone come out of darkness and into the light of the Lord. The camaraderie in a fighter squadron doesn't come close to the fellowship I have with believers!*

It wasn't always easy for me to lead people to Christ.

I really wanted my buddies I grew up with to share my new joy. I thought, *There is no way they are Christians. They are still doing the same old thing. I've got to try to reach them.*

I called one friend and said, "Hey, I'm in Birmingham. Let's get together."

"Great! Come on over to the house," he said. I drove over to his house and was just getting ready to start into the gospel when the phone rang. Another of my old friends was on the line.

"Frank, is here, come on over." A third friend dropped by and we had talked a little when one of the fellows said, "We've got enough for a game of poker. Where are your cards?"

"Hey, guys, I don't want to play poker. I want to tell you all what Christ has done in my life."

"Aw, Frank, we don't want to hear that. Deal the cards."

18

Alive at five

For the first time in my life, I felt truly free. I used to feel free only when I was doing things like flying or drinking. But as soon as it was over and I was by myself, I felt caged. Now the freedom came from inside me. God's Spirit was now living in my body in union with my human spirit and God had given me a new heart. He was working the changes in me that I had tried for so many years to make on my own.

I preached my new revelations to the little church in Oxford and they responded. One of the church members suggested I go see a lady in town whose husband was in the military in Okinawa. Saturday afternoon I went to see her and explained how she could trust in Christ. She became a believer and started coming to church.

One Sunday morning her husband was in church with her. That afternoon I dropped by to get to know him, but he had already left for his new assignment in North Carolina.

She told me that after she became a Christian she wrote and told him about what had happened in her life. She smiled, "He thought I had lost my mind, but I sent him Christian tracts and books. When he came home, I got him to church. He wouldn't take the truth from me, but he would have listened to you. I got him there, but you didn't tell him about Jesus." Tears filled her eyes, and she bit her lip.

Oh! I felt awful! I didn't remember what I had said that day, but obviously I didn't bring in the gospel or challenge people to accept Christ. I wrote the man and explained the gospel in the letter, but I never heard from him.

Since that day, every time I preach I always explain the gospel or bring the gospel in during the sermon. At the end I give people an opportunity to respond.

The second summer, I moved to Oxford to pastor full-time at Dodson Memorial for the three months I was not in seminary. It took awhile to move my books and stuff into the little parsonage, and I got to bed late. Before going to sleep I prayed, "Lord, I want you to wake me up tomorrow morning at the time you want me to get up for the rest of the summer. After tomorrow, I'll set my alarm for that time."

Morning dawned, and my eyes flew open. I looked at my watch. It was 5 a.m.

"Lord, you've got to be kidding! Five a.m. all summer?" I got up but fell asleep trying to pray and meditate on the Word. That night I prayed again, "Lord, I believe I auto-suggested myself into waking up so early. Let's do this one more time."

The next morning a light plane buzzed the parsonage. My eyes snapped open. It was 5 a.m.! I got up but again fell asleep on my Bible.

That night I asked, "Lord, did you send that pilot or did he do that on his own? Let's try this one more time!"

The next morning I woke up and looked at my watch. It was 5:05 a.m. Why 5:05?! I got up, this time making coffee first. When I read my Bible and prayed, I stayed awake. I really felt like God met me through His Word early in the morning.

About 8:00, I walked to a nearby restaurant for breakfast. There was a clock on the wall. My watch was five minutes fast!

"O.K., Lord. I give up."

For the rest of the summer I set the alarm for 5 a.m. and got up to meet God. The bookcase in the little church was stuffed with old books by men I had never heard of. I found some old, worn-out paperback books of Charles Spurgeon's sermons and wondered, *Who is Spurgeon?* I soon found out. I grew in my faith so much that summer.

An Army major and his family joined our Oxford church. While they were on vacation in Virginia, their only son, an eight year old, was killed when he was hit by a truck while riding his bicycle. After they came home, I went to see them.

"Frank," he said, "the pastor in Virginia explained that God didn't have anything to do with our son's death. God has set the world in motion, and He is not going to interfere. This has given me some peace. Don't you tell me that God had anything to do with my son's death, or I'll hate God."

"I'm sorry, Major, but I believe that preacher has given you a false peace. If God isn't going to interfere, what's the point of praying? Actually, the God of the Bible constantly interferes. Not a sparrow falls without Him. The thing to do is to turn to God and trust Him in this."

Several months before the accident, the major's wife had said to me, "My husband is not a Christian. I know he gives the right answers, but in his heart he's never turned to Christ. Please pray with me that God will do whatever He has to do to bring him to Himself."

The major did turn to the Lord and became a strong Christian. God gave them another child and now that family will all one day be in heaven. I saw again how the Lord guides us through circumstances, His Word and even tragedy.

That fall, back at seminary, Joe Lee discipled me in a

relaxed way. When I hit problems in classes, he would suggest helpful books to read. Once a month he would take me to a Christian bookstore to buy the biographies of great men and women of faith.

I read about George Müeller, who ran a huge orphanage on prayers; Hudson Taylor, who founded the China Inland Mission; William Carey, the father of modern missions; Amy Carmichael, a missionary to India; and many others.

As I read these biographies, I became more and more excited about reaching the world with the good news of Christ.

Joe took me to my first World Missions Conference. If there was a missionary visiting the seminary he said, "Let's take him to lunch and see how God directed him to the mission field."

I thought about being a missionary pilot but really felt a stronger call to pastor a church. I thought, *Surely God wants me to have a mission-minded church.*

God had used circumstances to guide me. He had used men like Joe and Dr. Gutzke to lead me to Him. All that summer, His Word became a light to direct my steps. Now I saw how reading about men and women who trusted God showed me how I too could follow Him. I would need to remember their stories and cling to the ways God would guide me. Life was about to get complicated.

19

Just for the summer

In my senior year at seminary, I was awarded a "fellowship" to do postgraduate work on a Ph.D. at a school of my choice. I didn't know the seminary gave fellowships; so I thought, *If I was given a fellowship after clashing theologically with a number of my professors, God must want me to do postgraduate work.* Therefore, I applied and was accepted at New York University.

After I graduated from seminary with two degrees, a Master of Divinity and a Master of Theology, the Birmingham Presbytery contacted me. They asked if I would organize a new church in Cahaba Heights, a fast-growing area of Birmingham.

"No," I told them, "I believe God wants me to do post-graduate work."

"Will you at least come for the summer to just help us get a church started?" they asked. "We have the funds to buy land and support the work until the new church grows."

"If you will allow me to take a foreign language at one of the universities in Birmingham to meet the language requirements for my doctoral study, I'll come. But just for the summer."

They didn't think this would be a problem, so I returned to Birmingham to begin my summer job.

The Cold War was raging. As America and Russia were at the height of the missile race, I armed myself with a census and started calling on families. There were many new homes around Cahaba Heights, but it was still fairly rural. Many people were interested in starting a new church. I was encouraged by the response and made plans to get it started.

Normally, a new church would start with a home Bible study. However, there were already enough people interested to have Sunday school and church services.

I asked the people I visited about their past experience in church. Had they taught Sunday school? Had they been a deacon or an elder? Did they play the piano? Also, I tried to get an idea of exactly where they were in their spiritual growth. When people sounded like they could help, I asked them to teach the children in Sunday school or work with junior high kids. There were enough people who were willing to commit themselves, so we started with a full-scale Sunday school and church.

We rented a vacant unit and a recently closed barber shop in a shopping center that had never prospered. Several people pitched in to build partitions to make rooms. In the barber shop, we put up curtain-rod partitions and gave the walls a coat of paint. Several churches in the area contributed things we needed. One gave some old green wooden chairs. Another gave an old rough-hewn pulpit and communion table. We were ready for God to stock the store with people.

Worship services began June 5, 1960. Seventy people attended the first Sunday. We had everything from a nursery to an adult Sunday school. Even though we had only four departments, we covered every age group.

The junior high and younger children met in the barber shop. To teach them, I used the story format I had learned when I taught the orphans. That experience had been great preparation for this. We had a lively piano player, and I led the singing using all my old "Wonder Book" camp songs. The kids had a good time, and I enjoyed working with them. The fact that they enjoyed

Sunday school was a big factor in getting the church started. If kids don't like church, parents will usually look for another place to worship.

We kept two guest books on a table at the front door. One was for those who wanted to become charter members and one was for folks "just visiting." The people who wanted to be charter members had to petition the Presbytery so we could become an official Presbyterian church. When we had enough people, a commission was appointed to examine the charter members, hold an election to choose officers and constitute the congregation as a church.

My goal was to help the church achieve that position. They could then call a pastor and my summer job would be over. I was looking forward to New York University.

I was surprised when they asked me to stay on as pastor. I told them I thought it was God's will for me to go back to school.

"Will you reconsider your decision? We really would like for you to stay on."

This shook my certainty about God's will and getting my doctorate. I wondered how God would guide me. Was I wrong about needing more schooling? It had seemed obvious that I should get my Ph.D. because of the unusual circumstances surrounding the fellowship. I realized I had not prayed about accepting the fellowship or staying on as pastor. I asked God to show me what to do.

I was still a 'weekend warrior' with the Naval Air Reserves and had to leave for a two-week duty flying out of the naval air station at Jacksonville, Florida.

I told the congregation, "I will pray about this while I'm gone and give you an answer when I get back." I was hoping God would guide me with another "star."

During those two weeks, I felt a growing certainty that God wanted me to stay on as their pastor. The doctoral fellowship was good anytime within five years. I would stay till the church was established, then go for my Ph.D.

September 25, 1960, Briarwood Presbyterian Church was officially chartered with ninety members, not counting children! One month later, I was installed as pastor. Three elders and six deacons were elected and the women's ministry was organized the same week. Our first year, 1960-61, we grew 78 percent.

It was an exciting time in history. We all gathered around the TV to watch as Alan Sheppard manned the first space flight. As the Berlin wall was going up in Germany, the walls in people's hearts in Birmingham were being torn down. Many were coming to Christ.

In a little while, our "storefront church" was packed. Sunday school classes increased and met in the dry cleaners, Valley Heating Company and every other available space. We met with people who wanted to join the church in the cleaners. Our joke was we took them to the cleaners.

None of us realized that this was only the beginning of a great work of God!

20

Paddle hard!

She's back! Barbara moved back to Birmingham during my first year with the church. I wondered how she felt about me. Would she still love me? I called her, feeling as nervous as a sixteen year old. "Would you go out to supper with me? I have so much I want to talk with you about."

We had not seen each other for three long years and talked nonstop. The hours passed like minutes. My eyes couldn't get enough of looking into hers. At the same time God had been changing my life, He had also been working in hers. She seemed, now more than ever, the woman I loved and wanted to marry. At supper, I took her hand and asked, "Why do you suppose God has brought us back together after all this time?"

"I don't know, but I don't want to take any major steps without knowing we are in His will." I understood her caution. I had hurt her before and didn't want to do it again.

"Can we seek God's will about marriage?" I asked. I was afraid of what she would say. It seemed like an hour before her eyes met mine. She looked at me. I tried to read her thoughts. Then a slow smile spread across her face. She dropped her eyes and said, "Yes."

Our dating was mostly going to Briarwood Church activities. My graceful ballerina brought a lot of class to the square dance in a church member's basement. Her charm and outgoing personality won many people's hearts at church picnics and retreats. I was more quiet and reserved. Barbara was the opposite. She would laugh and talk and hug everyone. She was the perfect complement for me. I was so glad to have her by my side.

On one church retreat in Pensacola, Florida, we went for a long walk, our feet squeaking on the powder-white sand. In the late afternoon, we sat in the edge of the blue-green water and watched the sun go down. It made a shining path of light over the water, like God had cracked opened the door to heaven. I proposed. She accepted. It seemed to me I had entered heaven's door. I don't remember our feet touching the sand as we hurried back to announce our engagement. No one was surprised. They rejoiced with us and gave me a lot of backslapping and hugs for Barbara. Our love for each other was obvious.

The next Sunday I announced our engagement to the church and added, "As you can see, I'll do anything to get a new member." There was one hitch in our wedding plans. Barbara said she would vow to "love and honor" her new husband, but she was not going to say she would "obey!" I said, "If you don't, we won't." After due consideration she agreed with the Christian vow to "love, honor and *obey*" her husband.

On November 3, 1961, Col. Joe Lee, my dear friend who led me to Christ, married us in "our" storefront church. Our decision of marrying and having the reception in the storefront horrified both our mothers. They wanted a much more attractive setting, like the beautiful old stone churches with their stained glass windows where we grew up. But, believe me, Barbara could make any place beautiful.

After the reception, I had planned an elaborate get-away. I thought my old buddies would chase us as I had done them. As we leaped into the car, Anita, Barbara's sister, slipped a note in her hand. I kept looking back to see the chase car, but no one followed. I guess they weren't sure how to handle a preacher.

In our haste, we didn't read the note from Anita until an hour later. The note was simply a verse of Scripture; "Seek ye first the kingdom of God, and His righteousness; and all these things shall be added unto you" (Matt. 6:33). We read it and prayed, asking God to let this be a theme verse for our marriage.

The mountains of North Carolina were ablaze with red and golden leaves. It looked like God's fireworks as we drove up the Blue Ridge Parkway. The air was chilly and we snuggled by the fire in our chalet. It was wonderful to be together. One day the manager let us use a canoe to paddle in the lake that was surrounded by woods. As we paddled, marveling at the beauty surrounding us, bright red and yellow leaves floated past the boat. We laughed and splashed each other with the paddles. Barbara leaned back, and I paddled her like a queen around the quiet lake.

Suddenly, I realized we had gotten into a strong current. Barbara sat up, looking around. I heard a noise that was unmistakable. We were heading for a waterfall! I struggled to turn the canoe around and paddle back upstream. I threw Barbara a paddle. The current was so strong we could not gain ground. I shouted, "PADDLE HARD!" Barbara turned around and looked at me with a hurt expression. "You spoke harshly to me," she whimpered. I didn't apologize but shouted back, "PADDLE!"

Somehow we made it back, but this was my first insight into the differences between us. I realized "they lived happily ever after" was only true in fairy tales. This was real life, and it more closely resembled our lake experience; smooth water laced with strong currents, sometimes even a waterfall.

21

No Prince Charming

"From a secret admirer." Barbara's dad would place such notes under the windshield wipers if he saw his wife's car in the parking lot. Her father was very romantic. He left love notes to her mother around their house. Barbara never remembered hearing her parents argue. Her dad helped around the kitchen and even brought his wife breakfast in bed.

I was not the Prince Charming she thought she had married. It shocked her when I would say, "What did you do that for!?" if she did something I thought was wrong.

She burst into tears, "You don't love me."

I was astounded. "What do you mean, I don't love you?"

"You don't write me any notes," she whimpered blowing her nose.

"Notes?"

I had a lot to learn.

Barbara helped me learn to have boundaries. Her wise advice has helped me make many choices that were hard for me.

Back when I was still in seminary and pastoring the church in Oxford, Alabama, I picked up a young hitch-hiker. He was headed for Memphis to get a job driving a truck. I knew it would take a long time to hitch that far, so I bought him a bus ticket. About a year later he wrote me a letter saying he was in prison outside Atlanta. I visited him and led him to Christ. I wrote follow-up letters and encouraged him to read the Bible. After he got out of jail, he came to Birmingham to see me and Barbara.

We got him a place to live and a job with one of our church members who was a veterinarian. He didn't like washing and caring for dogs, so he quit. He thought selling Fuller brushes would be more in line with his abilities. I set him up with a $500 suitcase of brushes. He worked several weeks before deciding that wasn't for him either. So I went around the neighborhood selling brushes.

Meanwhile, he got married and got a job ferrying cars for dealers. He would drive one to the Midwest, then go to California to ferry one elsewhere. He called me for money from California.

Barbara put her foot down after this happened a few times. "Frank, you are being an enabler to someone who will never stand on his own as long as you continue to bail him out. You're not helping him. He needs to learn to stand on his own two feet."

"You're right!" I said, seeing her wisdom. Then I got a call, "My wife is having a baby in the back seat of my car. We need $50 to get into the hospital!" Of course, I sent the money.

Finally, I had to tell him, "I'm not sending any more money." He couldn't believe it. It was hard for me to say no, but I knew Barbara was right.

Several years later, a Mayflower moving truck drove up to our home. It was the former hitchhiker, his wife and son (whom he had named for me). He was a driver for Mayflower, and they were doing great. Barbara was right. Once I quit bailing him out, he started acting responsibly!

One day a lady in our church asked me to feed her dog while she was out of town. She asked sweetly,

"Frank, would you mind going by my house on your way home and feeding my dog? I'll be gone all next week and I just can't put him in a cage at the vets. He would be so unhappy."

"Sure, I'll be glad to." When I came in after dark the third day Barbara was livid.

"I can't believe that woman asked you to feed her dog! Why on earth did you agree? You don't have time to do that."

"Well, she asked me. And I didn't see any reason why I couldn't. Her house isn't too far from the church." It seemed obvious to me that if someone asked for my help, there were enough hours in the day to fit it into my schedule, somehow.

As the church grew, I would need to learn to be more strategic with my time. Barbara helped me find a balance.

22

Old debts

Be sure your sins will find you out. I never realized that the things I had done in high school would come back to haunt me many years later.

After reading *New Testament Follow Up* by Waylon Moore, I was convinced of the need for teaching people who received Christ the basics of faith.

I prayed, "Lord, the next guy you let me lead to You, I'm going to follow up."

That week I shared Christ with an insurance salesman, and he accepted the Lord. I told him, "Jack, I want to help you grow in your Christian life. Let's meet every week to study the Bible. I'll give you some homework so you can also study on your own."

He was eager to get started, and we met Thursday evenings to study and pray. I gave him a fill-in-the-blank booklet that dealt with the basics of Christian life.

I had another man pray with me, and Jack also led a friend to Christ. I didn't have another free night, so I invited them to meet with Jack and me. All of a sudden I had a small group Bible study. I had never been in a group with new believers before, but immediately saw the value as these men began to grow spiritually. I wanted to multiply such groups in the church. This was the beginning of our Home Bible Class program.

One couple who came wanted to reach their neighbors but didn't think they would come to the Thursday night class. They said, "Our friends would come if we had a Bible class in our apartment complex. Would you teach it?"

"I don't have another night free, but how about my asking someone else to teach?" They agreed, so I asked one of the men in the class who had shown leadership to do it for me. This process continued until there were home Bible studies in many neighborhoods of our members. We offered training in how to lead the classes for those who had never done it before.

Here in the "Bible Belt," most of the churches were full of people. But most of them never read or understood the Bible. Like I had, they were trying to earn their salvation. Our Bible classes were like a wake-up call. For the first time, people began to understand how to have a personal relationship with God and walk with Him.

High school Bible classes met once a week after school in members' homes. It was a great way for our teenagers to reach their friends for the Lord.

For the younger kids, we started after-school Neighborhood Bible Clubs. These were led by several women in the church. One young girl who became a Christian in her neighborhood club is now in full-time Christian service. She was the only believer in her family. Reaching the children opened the door to reach the family for Christ.

The 12-14 year old girls club, led by Donna Green, started in our home with our daughter Anita and thirteen of her friends. It increased to sixty the first summer. This group grew into an interdenominational group and drew girls from public and private schools all over the city.

God planted a great desire in my heart to reach high school students who didn't go to church. But I had no idea how to go about it. One day while praying, I said "Lord, if there is anything in my life displeasing to you, show it to me. And, by your grace, I'll straighten it out."

The theft of $25 from my high school fraternity came

to mind. No way. I firmly believed the Lord didn't want me to dig up that old crime. Even if I could pay back the money, who would I send it to? That happened more than ten years ago. Besides, if I give them the money they wouldn't use it for anything good. The more excuses I made, the stronger the conviction grew that I should pay back the stolen money.

To get it off my mind, I prayed again. "Lord, if you really want me to give back the money, I'm willing. Lead me to someone in the fraternity, and I'll know for certain it's You leading me to do this."

The next day I was invited to a luncheon at the Birmingham Country Club. My old fraternity brother, Fred Taylor, was there, and we sat together. He asked, "Frank, have you received an invitation to the alumni banquet of the Sigma Fraternity?"

"No, I didn't get one," wishing he'd drop the subject.

Fred said, "See that fellow on the other side of the room? He's the treasurer of our old fraternity."

Great. Now I had to fulfill my promise to God. I went over and introduced myself and wrote down his name and address. When I got home, I wrote to the fraternity. "Dear Sigmas, In high school I was the treasurer of Sigma and stole $25. I know the Lord wants me to pay back the money. If you want interest on the money, please let me know.

"P.S. I'd appreciate your not publishing this letter in the Birmingham News." I signed my name, wrote a check, stamped and mailed the letter.

The next few days I read the paper carefully. I could just see "Extra, extra, Pastor is a thief!"

A few weeks later I received a phone call from one of the Sigmas. He asked if I would speak at their annual banquet. I couldn't imagine why they'd want me, but agreed. At the banquet I told them how I had found true freedom by trusting Christ. They were very responsive. Later they asked me to speak at their father/son banquet. They took a vote at their next meeting and named me an advisor for the group.

When I read in the newspaper that a pro football player, Bill Wade, was coming to speak for the Fellowship of Christian Athletes, I got an idea. "Barbara, let's invite the fraternity to our house for supper and then take them to hear Bill Wade!"

About thirty boys came for supper and went to the meeting. They were open to Bill's message, but I knew they needed more than a one-time shot. I went back to Barbara with another idea. "You know, I believe they would meet with us every week if we would feed them." She agreed, and we invited the boys to our house the next week.

At our first meal/meeting Barbara prepared food for thirty, basing her estimate on the number of boys who had gone to hear Bill Wade.

Ninety came! They came by the carloads until there were wall-to-wall boys and girls. The fraternity had decided to make a "rush party" out of our supper meeting and brought their dates. Barbara was in a panic. There would never be enough food to feed everyone! But as she served the dinner onto the plates, the pot didn't run out. It was a loaves and fishes miracle. Everyone had enough.

From that beginning, we met weekly all summer. We called those meetings "The Bible Talk Supper Club." That catchy name caught on. The whole thing started as an outreach to my old fraternity, but branched out to reach high school students from all over the city. The Bible Talk Supper Club continued for five years.

At that time there wasn't any kind of group in Birmingham like Young Life. A couple who were converted in our church and helped us with the Club were trained by Young Life. They took over the Club for Barbara and me, continuing what we had been doing.

One of the students said, "Mr. Barker, you put the Scripture into 'our' language and your examples make it so clear. I admire you for not being afraid to say what you believe or 'step on anyone's toes.' Your talks are like putting a puzzle together, and by the end, I can see the whole picture."

I appreciated that encouragement and praised God for convicting me of my high school thievery. Now my conscience was free.

23

Due time

"Frank, this is ridiculous. You can't give like you pledged and have children! There is no way we can increase our giving percentage again. If anything, we ought to decrease it!"

The church increased my salary after we were married. As I had pledged, I also continued to increase the percentage of my giving to the Lord each year. Because of this, there was very little money left to support my wife and two children who were born in less than two years. This became a point of tension between Barbara and me.

Our third baby was on the way, Barbara was exhausted from chasing two and thought it would be physically impossible to raise three. I comforted her by saying, "Sweetheart, God will give you three-baby grace."

As pledge time was approaching, Barbara rattled off our other needs. "Our car is in shambles!" she said. "And our third baby is due in April. The hospital charges $500, and the only money we will have is the $150 the Presbytery provides! There is no way to give the Lord more than we are already giving!"

It was true, our old car was so rusty around the door, water dripped in when it rained. The tires were slick, and the brakes barely worked. The windshield wipers smeared and streaked so badly I could hardly see where I was going.

Barbara threatened, "If you up the pledge this time, I am leaving! I am not going to do this anymore!"

What could I say? I knew she meant it, but I felt I couldn't break my promise to God. "Well, Honey, that's between you and God." I prayed, and when the time came to make the pledge commitment, she was willing to increase the percentage, but with many prophecies of financial doom and gloom!

In January, when that pledge began, Bill and Virginia Strange started coming to church. I met with him weekly as I did with all new believers to get them started in the Christian life.

It was raining as I drove to Bill's car dealership for our meeting. The towel I kept on the seat to mop up the drips that splattered my sleeve was soaked. "Lord," I prayed, "you've got to keep this car running. I can't afford to get it fixed. I don't even know how I'm going to pay the hospital bill when our new baby comes next month."

Bill and I went to lunch in his car, so he didn't know the shape mine was in. As we ate he said, "Frank, I want to give you something if you will let me give it to you on my terms."

"What's that?" I asked.

"I want to furnish you with a new car. Actually, it won't be yours. It is one of our demonstrators. We will pay the taxes, the insurance and the licenses. You just put gas and oil in it and drive it."

"I'll take your terms!" I said, amazed at the Lord's immediate answer to my prayer. I drove home in a brand-new, air-conditioned, white station wagon. I walked in the house, gave Barbara a bear hug, grabbed her hand and pulled her outside. "Honey, look what God has given us!"

"Oh! Look! It has baby blue upholstery," she said running her hand over the seat. "You mean it has power brakes and power steering and even power windows?"

Barbara got so excited she went into labor. We had to rush to the hospital. At least she got to ride on baby blue upholstery.

On the fourth day of her five-day stay, she started worrying. "Now, what are we going to do? How are we going to pay our bill?"

"What are you worried about?" I asked. "You don't get out of the hospital until tomorrow."

I didn't know where the money was coming from. But I had seen how God always provided for those who trust Him.

That afternoon Bill Strange called me and asked, "Are you going to be home? I have a check to bring you."

Bill had taken our old car, fixed it up and sold it. He brought me a check for $500 which, with the $150 insurance money, exactly paid our bill.

"The Lord did that!" Barbara shouted.

"Yes, He did!" I agreed.

When it came time to pledge again, she wanted to give everything we had! I had to hold her back!

I believe giving to the Lord is very important. I see people grow more spiritually as they take steps of obedience and faith in this area than in almost any other.

Barbara came from an affluent family who lived in Mountain Brook, a wealthy community in Birmingham. Her dad did not approve of my approach to giving. The first Christmas after we married, he gave her a sizable cash present. There was a great need in the church so I gave the money her dad had given her. He was furious. He lectured me, "If I am going to give money to the Lord, I will give it myself and take it off my income tax!" But through the years he saw God meet all our needs. It changed his perspective, too.

Barbara's greatest fear was that there would come a

day when I would give away all our salary. I didn't want her to ask her parents or anyone for help, because I didn't want people to think that Briarwood wasn't providing for us. We had a good salary but had chosen this lifestyle of giving. I felt God had called me to do this.

It was a hard lesson, but Barbara learned to trust the Lord for everything. One November there were doctor bills, the septic tank had broken and a lot of things were needed. But there was no money.

I believed it was imperative to pay our bills at the end of the month. We couldn't give away money that belonged to somebody else. We needed $600. Barbara thought she would get a check from the Steeple Arts Ballet Company where she taught. But the studio was audited, and all checks were held until the books were cleared.

I was supposed to go to California to speak to a big conference. She thought I would receive an honorarium to pay the bills. But a church member died, and I stayed home for the funeral.

Barbara directed weddings. She didn't ask for payment, but if people wanted to give her an honorarium, she accepted. She was helping with two weddings that month and hoped this would supply some of our needs. One person gave her a fruit basket and the other a crystal dinner bell. Every time she thought there would be some money coming in, it fell through.

"God is the source of our supply, not the teaching or speaking. Just look to God." I reminded her.

During the last week of November Barbara prayed, "God, I don't know what you are trying to do with us, but I need some encouragement if you want us to keep on giving the way we are."

"Be not weary in well doing. In *due* time you will

reap if you faint not," came to her mind. "Due time" meant the end of the month when bills were due.

The next Sunday I was preaching on Psalm 103. The verse "Bless the Lord, O my soul; and all that is within me, bless His holy name." Barbara took that as her instruction from the Lord. She thought, "My job is to bless God!"

Driving home from church she believed she was getting ready to see a miracle. What God was going to do for us had to happen soon because every bill must be paid by Friday. That meant her checks had to be in the mail by Thursday.

Monday morning she taught a Bible study and told the women, "This time next week, I'm going to tell you about a miracle."

The women asked, "What are you talking about?"

"I don't know what I'm talking about, but I'll know next week. I'll tell you then," Barbara said.

Tuesday, she awoke really nervous. What if God didn't send us the money! In her quiet time she prayed, "Lord, let there be something in the mailbox just to let me know you are there. I don't doubt you, but I need encouragement. Please, let there be something in the mail."

Later that day, she walked out to the mailbox and quickly shuffled through the junk-mail searching for her "encouragement." There was a postcard with a penny pasted on it. She believed God was saying, "I'm going to do it. I'm here."

Wednesday night Barbara went to choir practice. Tom Leopard, the church administrator, stuck his head in the door during rehearsal and signaled her to come out to see him. She put her music down and slipped out.

"Stop by my office after choir. Someone left a letter for you," he said.

She immediately thought, *Oh, there it is!*, then remembered not to look at things, but to the Lord. She wouldn't put her hope in a letter.

After choir practice she hurried around to Tom's office. He said, "A lady came by the church and handed this envelope to me and asked if I could get it to you."

Barbara tore it open and pulled out a package wrapped in yellow legal size paper. Six one hundred dollar bills fell into her hands. Tears welled up in her eyes. She looked at Tom and asked, "Who was the lady?"

"I don't know. She didn't tell me her name."

Barbara took the money home and got the children out of bed. "Come into the living room, kids." They gathered around the coffee table and watched wide-eyed as she opened the letter. She counted the bills as she spread them out on the table. They all laughed with joy and thanked the Lord for providing.

When all the bills were paid there was $100 left over. She had added wrong! Our bills were only $500, and there was $100 extra going into December when there were presents to buy.

I don't think everyone should live the way we do, but it was exciting for us to trust God. The only way to learn to trust Him is to depend on Him for something every day. For us, it was simply food.

It became our way of life. Barbara and the children learned to wait patiently on God. He always provided. We never lacked. We agreed to never tell anyone about our needs.

I said, "Briarwood takes good care of us. If we ever say we have a need, it would make the church look bad. Gossips would say the church doesn't take good care of their preacher. So nobody can know our needs but God."

When the children were old enough to understand,

they joined in prayer for the family's needs. It was a faith builder for them to watch God in time and on time, over and over again, provide just the amount of money we needed. He always provided whatever was needed.

24

Green chair prayer

"Frank, a wonderful Christian family wants to join the church, but they want to talk to you first."

Wednesday nights the deacons and elders visited folks in our area. Bob Barnes was one of the deacons and he and his partner came back excited about a family they had met.

"All right, I'll make an appointment and go see them when we visit next Wednesday." I went to see the family, and they were interested in our church. As I talked to them, I discovered they were not Christians. When I explained the gospel, they accepted the Lord. When the men came back to report on their visitation, I told them about this family coming to Christ.

Bob was very quiet.

All the next week, he worried about his own salvation. He reasoned, "I went to see those folks and thought they were Christians. The preacher called on them and he said they weren't. So, what is a Christian? ... maybe I'm not a Christian!"

Bob got so worried about his salvation that he came to see me. He said, "Frank, I'm not sure I'm a Christian. It has been worrying me ever since you led those folks to the Lord."

"Well, let's talk about it," I said and went through the gospel with him. He, like me years before, didn't know salvation was a gift. He believed if he was good enough God would let him into heaven. When he understood, he willingly accepted Christ and was relieved. Now he *knew* he was a real Christian.

Just as Joe, the Air Force Chaplain, had done with me, I gave him a biography of a great Christian to read. He read it and the next Sunday shook my hand and left a twenty-dollar bill in my palm.

"Get some more of those books and spread them around!"

A few weeks later he said, "Frank, I want to learn to pray. Will you help me?"

"The only way I know how to learn to pray is ... to pray! Let's get together every week and do it." I pulled out my little calendar and we set a day and time. We decided to meet in the storefront.

In our first meeting Bob asked, "What are we going to pray about?"

"Well, as I visit around the community, I have trouble talking about Christ. I can talk about the weather, politics, football, almost any subject, but I have trouble getting on the subject of the Lord Jesus. Let's pray that I'll be able to do that."

The next week God answered that prayer. I had eighteen opportunities to share the gospel, and it was easy to get into in-depth conversations about the Lord. Some of the people were already Christians. They joined the church. Others accepted the Lord and came to church.

As new people visited the church, Bob and I prayed for them. When they accepted the Lord, we invited the men to join our prayer group. Soon we had eight men meeting with us every week.

A man named Hilton, who visited the church, came to talk with me about several problems. "I don't have all the answers," I told him, "but God does. We need to pray for God to show you what to do."

"Prayer!" he blurted out. "I don't much believe there is a God! And I know He doesn't answer prayer."

"We've got a group that meets every Wednesday evening and we've seen some remarkable answers to prayer. How about coming and sitting in on the group?"

He came. The first thing he said was, "I don't want to be here under false pretenses. And I don't want to be a hypocrite. I don't believe in what you all are doing, but I'd like to. I just don't believe God answers prayer, but I really would like to believe it. I wish you all would help me."

Bob said, "Many of us were once in the same boat, but we have seen God answer our prayers."

"Frank also told me you men pray for specific things and get specific answers to your prayers," Hilton said. "Will you do that again and let me watch?"

"Sure!" I said.

"Okay," Hilton said. "Here is my request. Since attendance is off, I want you to pray that God will fill the church next Sunday."

"But this is the middle of the summer," one man said. "Everyone's on vacation."

Hilton wasn't about to be put off. "There are plenty of other people out in the community who aren't going to church," he countered. "Why don't you ask God to bring them? I want you to pray that the church will be filled this Sunday," he said, raising his chin and thumping a fist on his knee.

We could see Hilton was sincere and wasn't just being pig-headed about prayer. He had a valid prayer request. I said, "We need some sort of measuring stick to determine what you mean by 'filled,' Hilton."

"'Filled' means the ushers will have to bring out the green chairs from the barber shop," he said.

The "green chairs" were the painted wooden chairs given to us when we first began the church. We only used them for crowded services on Easter and Christmas. In effect, he was asking God for an Easter crowd in the middle of summer.

We all knelt and prayed for a miracle. After the "Amen" Hilton said, "You have to promise not to tell anybody about this prayer. Also, don't ask more people to come to church than you normally would during a week."

Sunday morning, I surveyed the congregation from the back of the storefront to see how many were there. The church wasn't two-thirds full. I was discouraged when I went to the pulpit to open the service with prayer. I peeked while I was praying and saw a lot of cars turning into the parking lot. In my heart I asked, "Lord, can it be?" As soon as I finished my unusually long prayer, the ushers let the latecomers in. To my amazed delight, the room was filled.

"I see the ushers are bringing in the green chairs," I announced and looked straight at Hilton. He was astonished as were the eight other men in the prayer group. (Those chairs became a symbol of God's faithfulness. Years later we brought one out of storage and placed it on the altar during one of our pledge campaigns for the new church on Highway 459.)

Needless to say, Hilton became a Christian and joined the prayer group. He was a strong believer and now awaits us all in heaven with our Lord.

Here again was another guiding "star." God led me through circumstances, people and His Word. Now I saw how He guided and directed not only me, but the whole church through prayer. It was fantastic to kneel with those men in the storefront before the God of heaven. He constantly amazed us as He answered our prayers. He answered our "important" prayers. But He also heard the prayer of a man who needed to see that God was listening even to the "small" things.

25

Ph.D. and diapers

Time was running out. I had to make a decision soon about using the fellowship I received in seminary for postgraduate work. I would lose it if I didn't. The five-year limit was almost up. What should I do?

The church had grown so much! Soon after the "green chair" miracle, we built a new building on the land bought by the Birmingham Presbytery. We constructed a large fellowship hall, Sunday school rooms, nursery and a kitchen. The fellowship hall was used for church services. Everyone was delighted to move into a real church building.

With three children, life was getting more and more complicated. I needed guidance. I had been praying about it, but I still wasn't sure what God wanted me to do.

Remembering how God had used godly men to direct me, I turned to Dr. Robinson. He had been one of my seminary professors. I made an appointment and drove to see him in Atlanta.

"Why do you want your Ph.D.?" he asked. "Do you think God wants you to be a college or seminary professor?"

"No, Sir," I replied. "I believe I'm supposed to be a pastor."

"Then why do you want a Ph.D.?"

"Well," I said, "I'm speaking to a sophisticated audience. There are doctors, lawyers, businessmen and educators. If I had a Ph.D. behind my name, it would give more credibility to what I preach."

"Oh, young man!" he sat up in his chair and looked

as if I had committed blasphemy. "The Holy Spirit convicts men of sin, not your degrees!"

I forgot about the Ph.D. and went home.

The thing for which I most needed a Ph.D. was how to be a husband.

When the third baby was born, Barbara went into what the doctors called "postpartum" depression. I knew it was really "Frank Depression."

I never helped around the house like her father had done. We had three babies in two and a half years. I didn't change a diaper with the first two and didn't feel the least bit guilty. I thought that was *her* end of the baby.

It was no wonder that the sweet thing I married turned mean. However, I didn't realize my own problem. She was the problem, I thought. I was baffled and didn't know what to do. So I prayed, asking God for wisdom.

One day I picked up the book *Calvary Road* and read the chapter "Revival in the Home." The author took I Corinthians 13 and applied it to husband/wife relationships. After reading that book, I understood that I was the biggest part of Barbara's problem. "No wonder she was depressed. I have been the opposite of what this said. I haven't loved her the way I should." I decided I would love my wife with God's kind of love by His grace. That was the hardest thing I ever tried to do in my life!

I thought back to when I flew fighter jets. One time I had such a bad case of vertigo, I was sure that I was flying upside down. My instruments told me that I was flying right side up. I stared unbelievingly but knew I had to trust the instruments. If I had believed my feelings and disregarded the gauges, I would have crashed.

Learning to love Barbara unconditionally, even when she was angry, was like flying by my instruments. All my emotions would want to yell and be angry. The Bible, my control panel, told me to react in kindness.

Late afternoons were the hardest for Barbara. A home with little children is chaos from 5:30 to 6:30 p.m. The piranha hour, some people call it. The kids are hungry, tired and sleepy. Supper has to be cooked, children fed, bathed, stuffed into their pyjamas and put to bed. When I got home, Barbara would snap, "You're late."

"I tried to phone, but the line was busy."

"The kids must have knocked it off the hook. They are asleep on the floor."

"I will wake them up."

"Supper is cold", her tone of voice was as cold as the supper.

"I'll heat it up", I said trying to stay calm.

"This is the third time this week you've been late", she accused. I couldn't deny it. But my endurance was overtaxed.

"Shut up!" came out before I could look to the Lord for help. The second that came out of my mouth I ran into the bathroom. It was the only place to get away from our dogs and kids. On the cold, hard tile I fell on my knees and prayed, "God, I blew it. I did not treat my wife with love. Please forgive me. Fill me with Your love so I can love her like I should."

Back in the kitchen I told her, "I was not loving to you. I didn't treat you in a kind way."

"That's right," she said. "You really didn't treat me in love."

"You're not so loving yourself," I snapped.

I hurried back to the bathroom to my knees again.

This kind of "conversation" went on, from my perspective, for about a month and a half. When I reacted badly, I asked her, "Please forgive me. I didn't treat you in Christ's love."

One day she responded, "No, you forgive me. I didn't treat you with Christ's love."

A miracle was happening between us! We both started asking forgiveness when we offended the other. Our marriage began to blossom. God's pattern works!

I made an effort to find out what her needs were because I wanted to love her as Christ loved the church. Since Barbara's family had openly expressed affection, I knew I needed to openly demonstrate my love.

My family had been loving, but not physically expressive. Early in our marriage I *might* acknowledge her presence if she came into a room with a lot of people. To show her my love, I knew I should put my arm around her and give a kiss on the cheek. But with my reserved upbringing, this made me feel like I had taken my clothes off in public.

One day I decided to give the open affection a try. Clinching my teeth, I "took off my clothes in public." With deliberate steps, I walked over to her. I put my arm around her waist and pecked her cheek. I was so embarrassed. But after several times, it didn't seem so bad. In fact, I began to enjoy it.

My efforts to demonstrate affection became so great that if she was going down the hall and I was going the other way, I just wouldn't let her pass. I would grab her and bend her backward with a kiss.

The children heard us and came from everywhere giggling, "Hug us, too! Hug us, too!" Even the dogs came running and barking. Everyone responded to our demonstration of love.

Once when we were on vacation and eating in a restaurant, Barbara looked around and saw other couples talking very animatedly. I was not saying anything. Barbara was talking but got quiet as she thought, "My goodness, we don't have a marriage. Look at all these other couples. We don't have anything to say to each other. Our marriage is falling apart."

I paid the bill and as we walked outside, I put my arm around her and said, "Isn't it wonderful. We can be together and not even have to talk?" That's when Barbara told me what she had been thinking. That was another lesson in communication for me. Women need words.

I realized as a couple we needed to develop an interest in each other's activities. The couple that plays together stays together. But Barbara's main interest is ballet. I wasn't about to take up ballet, but I could be interested in what she was doing and be her biggest cheerleader.

26

50/50

A few years after we built our fellowship hall, Sunday school rooms and kitchen on the ten acres adjacent to Highway 280 south, we built a sanctuary with 1,000 seats. More people came until there was no room in the parking lot. The side of the highway was the only place folks could park.

If some doctors in our congregation had not revived the driver whose car was hit when he was coming into the church parking lot, we would have had a funeral instead of a church service. The near-fatal accident convinced us that something must be done about our parking lot.

At the next Saturday morning prayer group, Hilton Piper prayed, "Lord, I ask that within two weeks, work will have begun on the new parking lot."

There was no way in the world I saw that this could happen. I quickly tried to amend his prayer, but several other men began agreeing with him.

The only land we owned was a hill with a deep slope and a creek at the bottom. The price of moving the hill into the hole was more money than we could pay.

A committee had been appointed to study the parking situation. However, it wasn't scheduled to give the report for ten days. Bids had to be taken, a contract approved and money raised. There wasn't enough time to get all that done in two weeks.

By the next Saturday prayer meeting, nothing had happened. The gist of our prayers went like this, "Lord, one more week."

Monday night I was at a friend's home, and a lady from the church asked me a lot of questions about the proposed parking lot. I didn't tell her about our prayer but did say the committee was working on it.

"I want to make a contribution of $5,000," she said. "I'll send the money to the church this week."

At the Session meeting Tuesday night, the parking lot chairman gave his report. "Our committee contacted the architect and got his recommendations. We also took the liberty of getting some bids. We wanted to include them in our report tonight so you would be aware of the amount of money we need to raise. The lowest bid is $5,000."

"The Lord has answered prayer!" I told them about Hilton's prayer and the lady's $5,000 donation.

"More good news," the chairman said. "The contractor with the lowest bid is between jobs and can start work immediately!"

"It is the will of God!" a Session member shouted.

On Thursday, bulldozers were moving trees and dirt. God had answered with two days to spare because one man believed God answers prayer.

Most churches, including ours, are afraid that if they start a missions program, they can't build needed buildings. Man! Did we need buildings! All our space was maxed out.

Giving generously to missions had been one of those guiding "stars" God had planted in my heart back in seminary. Since the beginning of Briarwood, the elders and I set a goal to give half of the money to work beyond our church. For every dollar we spent on ourselves, we would give a dollar to home and world missions, mercy ministries, and the planting of new churches.

It took seven years to reach that goal. There have been a

few times since then that we couldn't make that 50/50 split. But over the years, the goal has been a strong motivation to be especially careful in how we plan the budget. Because of that planning, millions of dollars have been given to other ministries.

I wanted Briarwood to be mission-minded and tried to pass on the importance of giving to missions. I knew the battle for missions is won or lost in the local church. That's where missionaries find financial and prayer support. The local church should also be the recruiting station for home and foreign missions. The possibilities of what a church can do in missions is unlimited.

At first the Session argued that we couldn't afford to support even one missionary family. It cost $6,000 a year in the 1960s, and that seemed like an impossible sum. We needed new buildings for Sunday school, salaries for new staff and our ongoing programs took a lot of money.

We learned that one church usually didn't undertake the total support of a missionary, but even partial support was a sizable task for us. In 1964, we expanded our missions program from a general "once a year offering" and invited a missionary couple to come for a weekend conference. An offering was taken, and it amounted to $300. The church was small, but it wasn't that small!

At the next Session meeting I said, "I think the reason the offering was so small is the members didn't get personally involved with the missionaries. Let's take another approach. I think we should contact an independent faith mission board. Let's get a young couple who have finished their training and are ready to go to the field but lack financial support. If the congregation pledges enough money for one year, the couple can go on to the field."

We prayed for God's guidance and asked, "Give us a couple who will identify with our congregation." In the meantime, I read a book that explained how churches should take a separate pledge for missions apart from their regular budget. "Lord," I prayed, "that sure is different from the usual way. I'll give copies of this book to the Session, but You'll have to convince them to try it."

The book stated that churches who gave priority to missions experienced an increase in their whole stewardship program. They were able to care for their needs as well as give to missions.

We timed our next year's conference with our assigned couple's completion of three months jungle training in Mexico. The week started out with problems. The conference was to begin Thursday. Monday, the missionaries called from Mexico and said, "We wrecked our car, and it's going to take four days to get it fixed. Do you want us to fly up there?"

My engineer training came in handy as I did some quick mental arithmetic. We definitely could not fly them up. "Stay where you are. Get the car fixed and try to make the last day of the conference. We have another couple who can carry on until you get here."

Did they listen? No. Using all their savings for plane tickets they flew to Birmingham arriving before noon on Thursday.

As the conference approached, we realized we had made a critical error in scheduling. It fell on Spring Break; everyone would be on vacation.

We had a wonderful conference with a handful of people. Saturday night Barbara and I went home completely discouraged. We had to raise $6,000 for this missionary couple by Sunday evening.

Barbara and I hit our knees. I prayed, "Lord, I don't see how you can pull any good out of our mess. I'm just going to open my Bible, and if You want to give me a word of encouragement, I really would appreciate it."

Barbara raised her head and looked at me puzzled. That's not the way I usually sought guidance, but I was desperate. My Bible fell open to Psalm 92.

"It's a good thing to give thanks unto the Lord and sing praises to the Most High."

"Are You telling us, Lord, that we can thank You and praise You; that You are going to do this thing?"

The next verse said, "To show forth Thy loving kindness in the morning and Thy faithfulness every night."

"In other words, Lord, we won't have the whole $6,000 at the end of the morning service, but by the end of the night service, You will have shown Yourself faithful."

I read on, "For Thou Lord has made me glad through Thy work, I will triumph in the works of Thy hand." Peace about the money descended on our hearts. We believed those verses were our word from the Lord.

At the eight o'clock service $2,000 was pledged. At the 11:00 service $3,000 was pledged. Folks who had been out of town came to the evening service, and I announced, "We need $1,000 to complete the pledge. If you haven't made a pledge yet, you may still do so."

A final pledge was taken and the folks dismissed. After church, there were three couples who went out to eat with the missionaries. We all waited anxiously as Tom, the chairman of the missions committee and a banker, added up the pledges. He put down his pen. Surprise and delight lit up his face. He exclaimed, "$6,367.00!"

We didn't know whether to laugh or cry!

"Wait a minute," Tom inquired. "Why would there be $367 extra dollars?" He looked at the missionaries and asked, "How much did your plane tickets cost?"

"$367!" they exclaimed through their happy tears.

We were all laughing and hugging each other! Everyone in the restaurant turned around to gawk at us.

"Let's thank Him now," I said - and we did - not caring what other diners thought. How exciting it was to see the Lord's faithfulness!

That small beginning seemed big at the time. It launched our World Missions Conferences. Many churches only give money to their denominational missionaries. But God has greatly blessed us in many ways as we give both to our denominational ministries and other missionaries in need of support. We have supported many ministries and parachurch organizations in the United States and overseas. In return, they have sent us their disciples and leaders who have helped our church. The church has never lost money because of this. The more we give, the more we seem to have.

We started teaching English classes to internationals to reach them with the gospel. There are hundreds of international students studying in Birmingham and a million in the universities in America. The mission field has come to us. If one in twenty becomes a Christian and goes back home, that would be 50,000 new missionaries.

27

I need help

That enlisted man who held up the crossed wands in the fog never left my mind. Fifteen years later, I thought about how he stood in the dark holding up his wands in a cross. He risked his own life and saved mine.

Since I had become a Christian, I had found the freedom I always wanted. But I knew that so many people in the world were like I was in that jet ... thinking they are fine, but heading toward fiery death. I wanted to stand like that man and hold up the cross of Christ so everyone could have the opportunity to be saved. But I realized that I couldn't do it by myself.

Christ commanded us to take His gospel, the good news about salvation, to everyone in the world. We call this the Great Commission. Jesus commissioned us as His ambassadors to speak for Him to the world.

Like that enlisted man on the airfield, every Christian should hold up crossed wands to point people to God.

I didn't come to this conviction from my seminary training, but later in my study of the Scriptures. It was another of the "stars" God used to guide me in leading my church. I noticed that the people involved in personal evangelism were more excited about God than other Christians who didn't share their faith.

How could I teach Briarwood members to share their faith?

Since our church began, men have gone with me to "visit" new people who came to church. First we met for dinner and prayer, and then went out in teams of two. At the end of the night, everyone met back to tell what happened. Listening to the reports, I realized the men didn't have any trouble "visiting," but they were not sharing Christ.

One of our men who went out every week asked me to write out what I said to lead people to the Lord. I did and they tried to learn it, but it was hard for them to remember. I think they weren't convinced they could lead people to Christ. That's what preachers do.

A young couple joined the church who had been led to Christ by the regional director of Campus Crusade for Christ at Georgia Tech. They said he regularly led students to the Lord and invited me to go to Atlanta to meet him. I thought this might be my answer to how to train the church to share Christ.

Jon and I hit it off. I was impressed with Campus Crusade's evangelistic material and training. I asked him, "Have you ever taught this at a church?"

"Yes, we've taught it a few times, but not on a regular basis."

We set a date, and the first Lay Institute for Evangelism in Alabama was held at Briarwood. The director brought fifteen people who helped with the training. They told stories of how they led people to Christ. We had 100 members who came to the training. The Crusade team did more in that one weekend to get my people sharing their faith than I had done in three years!

We started regular training in how to lead a person to Christ using the small booklet published by Campus Crusade for Christ, entitled *The Four Spiritual Laws*. Once a year we had a weekend Lay Institute for Evangelism, and hundreds of people came for the training.

Now everyone was able to lead their friends to the Lord. It wasn't just the pastor's job anymore.

One day I got a phone call from an oral surgeon in our church, Dr. Bill Buck. He took our Crusade training and regularly led friends, patients and even strangers to the Lord.

He said, "I just led an old buddy of yours to Christ."

"Great!" I said. "Who was it?"

"Fred Taylor. He came by to sell me some insurance, and I went over the Four Spiritual Laws with him. He prayed to receive Christ. I thought you would want to know since you two go way back."

"Yes, we were high school fraternity brothers. My sister, Minnie Lee, told me recently that I should share Christ with him. But I thought he was so set in his wild ways that he wouldn't be interested."

"Well, he fell into the kingdom when I presented the gospel," Bill said.

I had a hard time believing Fred was really converted and didn't even call him up. About two weeks later, I came back to my office after lunch, and Fred was waiting for me.

He looked me in the eye and asked, "Why didn't you tell me about Jesus?"

I could have sunk into the floor. "Fred," I said, "I tried to tell some of the old gang, and they wouldn't listen."

"I might not have listened either, but I deserved the chance!"

"You're right! Will you please forgive me?" I felt so bad!

"I forgive you. Now, let's go get the rest of our old buddies."

One by one we took them to lunch, and many came to Christ.

Fred led his family to the Lord, and they all joined the church. One day Fred asked me to do something for him. After a week or so, he called to ask if I had done it. "Yes, I did it," I told him, but I really hadn't.

"You lied to Fred," echoed in my mind as soon as I hung up the phone.

I picked up the phone and called him back.

"Fred, this is your pastor. I just lied to you."

One time of doing that cured me from lying.

28

Dancing in the church

Profits were up at Mark Fitzgerald's furniture. It was expanding its stores and Bailey Marks was turning his family business into a thriving company. His wife, Elizabeth, approached Barbara one afternoon and asked if I could get Bailey to go on church visitation with me.

"Honey," she told me that evening, "Elizabeth wants you to ask Bailey to go with you on visitation so he can learn to share Christ. Will you take him with you?"

Bailey hadn't come to our training in evangelism. I was doubtful. "Sweetheart, Bailey is so shy he would never do that, but I'll ask him." To my amazement he agreed to go.

I prayed, asking God to give us a good experience as we went out. At 8 p.m. we called on a businessman who had visited the church, and about 9:30 p.m. he invited Christ into his life. At 10:30 p.m. we had another appointment with a medical student after he finished studying. At 12:30 in the morning he got on his knees with us and committed his life to the Lord.

Bailey was ecstatic! It wasn't long before he came to me and said, "I believe God wants me in full-time ministry." The joy of seeing people's lives changed was worth more to him than all the money he was making as a successful businessman. He went on staff with Campus Crusade for Christ as special assistant to the founder and president, Dr. Bill Bright. After a year Dr. Bright told Bailey, "We don't have any work in Asia except in Korea. I'm putting you in charge of Asia. I want you to recruit some people, move there and start the work."

Bailey recruited two couples from our church: Bud and Elizabeth Newbold and Dr. Sam and Mary Glynn Peeples. Elizabeth Newbold had led the Peeples and Marks to the Lord in a home Bible class. Together they set up a training program in the Philippines. They also traveled to the various countries in Asia recruiting people to come to the Philippines for a year of staff training. The trainees returned to their own country to start a Campus Crusade ministry.

I went to Asia ten years later and traveled around with Bailey and Bud. They had 1,400 national staff in 28 countries. In Korea, I preached the gospel to millions who stood in the rain on Yoida Island during Explo '74. My "shy" friend, Bailey, went on to head up all of Campus Crusade's work outside the United States which involved 20,000 staff.

So many of our church members were learning to share their faith. They were always devising new ways to reach out to their friends and neighbors. Barbara came to me with an idea of her own.

"I don't know, Sweetheart. A preacher's wife teaching dancing?"

Barbara was a trained ballerina. She had run into her old ballet teacher who had asked her to come back and teach.

"Frank, you're always talking about reaching out to others, but I'm surrounded by Christians. If I teach, it would give me a lot of contact with girls with whom I could share."

"If you think God is leading you, go ahead. I'm sure no one will put your picture in The Birmingham News in your black tights."

She did and they did! Everyone in Birmingham got to see my wife leaping through the air in her black tights.

We both nearly died of embarrassment. But somehow, we survived the press.

However, it turned into a great ministry for Barbara. Taking the girls to lunch, Barbara was able to share Christ with them. I got used to my home being filled with skinny ballerinas coming to Bible study.

Another lady began a ballet program at Briarwood. When she became pregnant and quit, Barbara took over. It thrived under her leadership. She took C. S. Lewis' story, "The Lion, the Witch and the Wardrobe," which portrays the gospel in a unique and powerful way, and made it into a ballet.

A few years later, she developed a performing company, Ballet Exaltation. The total program has about 500 girls from four to eighteen years old. The Exaltation group of about ten travels to various overseas mission fields. They perform for audiences our missionaries engage. The company has proven to be a marvelous way to share Christ and disciple the dancers.

It is amazing to me that some people think if they give their lives to God, He will take away all their fun. The drive and desires in us are usually God-given. He didn't take away Barbara's passion for dance and performance. He set her free to use it in a way that was not only fulfilling for her, but glorifying to Himself.

29

One person a month

It was a big goal! It was more people than all the previous years combined. It happened during our church officer's retreat when we were discussing God calling folks from the church into missions. "We've prayed and asked God to call people, but we haven't set any goals," one of the elders said.

After praying, we came to a consensus. We would ask God to call at least one person a month from our congregation to go into full-time ministry either in the States or overseas.

Every Sunday I began to pray from the pulpit, "Lord, we as a congregation are asking you to raise up one person a month from our church to go on the mission field this year."

No one even blinked. Since members had learned they could lead people to the Lord and were actively doing it every week, many of them wanted to do it full-time.

Every time our officers met, we prayed on our knees for God to call men and women to the mission field from our congregation. Other church groups echoed this prayer.

Thirteen people went that year.

We were so excited we asked for more the next year. We prayed for fifteen to go from our church. Seventeen went! The next year we asked for twenty-one. Twenty-two went!

I preached at a missions conference in Jackson, Mississippi, and asked the pastor, Don Patterson, if there was anything he wanted me to emphasize.

"This church is 137 years old. In all those years, only four men have become pastors, but no one from here has ever gone to the mission field," he explained. "I'd like you to give this congregation a vision to go into the mission field."

I told him about our church praying, setting goals and asking God to raise up missionaries from our congregation.

Nine years later, Don spoke at Briarwood's missions conference. He told me that the day after our conversation, he asked his church staff to set a goal and ask God to raise up missionaries from their church.

He asked the men, "How many are you prepared to trust God to call out of our congregation this year?"

"Thirteen," was the unanimous response.

"Thirteen?" questioned Don. "In 137 years no one has gone. Not one! Are you sure you're prepared to ask God to raise up thirteen? We're talking about one year!"

Fourteen went. In the next nine years that church sent fifty-four missionaries to the mission field with Mission to the World, the Presbyterian Church in America mission arm.

Things did not always go so smoothly. At times it was very difficult pastoring a rapidly growing church. A friend recently asked me to tell some of my hardships in the ministry. Barbara answered for me. "When he flew to Asia to travel with Bailey Marks, he took a change of underwear. The rest of his suitcase was filled with MAALOX!"

People are always in need in a big church. I wanted to be available day or night to help in any way possible. I have cleaned up bathrooms after suicides and been at the bedside of many dying friends. It is not often that the phone is quiet at our house.

Lack of sleep has caused much embarrassment for Barbara and me. She finally quit singing in the choir after someone remarked that it was so kind of her to pray for me during my sermons. Barbara wasn't sure if that person was joking or not. On many Sundays, she bowed her head in the choir loft behind the pulpit and slept through the service.

Several times I have fallen asleep while counseling friends. One close friend, Jane Anderson, who is in charge of the Community Bible Study for women, came to me for advice. My head jerked up after nodding forward, and I found myself alone in my office. I wondered how long I had been asleep. I looked around groggily and noticed a note on my desk. It read, "Frank, thanks for the advice." Jane laughed about her counseling session with me for years.

I think one of my biggest embarrassments was at a large banquet. As I finished speaking, I told everyone I wanted to introduce the person who stood by my side, understood and helped me. Barbara was seated at the head table. She smiled, embarrassed at the obvious compliment, and twisted her napkin nervously. I went on and on with my praise and concluded dramatically. "This lady has been my right arm. I want you all to meet..." Barbara got ready to stand, "my secretary, Marilyn Beard," I concluded with a broad smile.

Barbara wouldn't speak to me for a week! She is such a wonderful complement to my personality. She is vivacious and bubbly and has never met a stranger. She talks with ease with anyone. I, on the other hand, am mostly quiet. I don't carry conversations easily.

While speaking at a banquet in Chattanooga, I was seated next to a woman who listened to my sermon tapes regularly. I was very tired and was silent through most of the meal. Later I was informed that the woman cried because she thought I didn't like her and wouldn't talk to her.

I know that I didn't arrive at my position as pastor of Briarwood by my winsome personality. If God can use me to accomplish things for His kingdom, He can use anyone. It is amazing whom God will use. When a person completely gives everything over to Him, God will do even "greater things than these."

I agree with Paul who said in Corinthians, "God chooses the weak things of the world to shame the things that are strong and the foolish to shame the wise so that no man can boast before God."

I could never boast. God has done it all!

30

Red and yellow, black and white they are precious in His sight

"I feel so clean! I feel so clean!" Lois said as we walked out of the third and final store.

I nodded, remembering how I had "come clean" after paying back the $25 I had stolen years before.

Before surrendering her life to Christ, Lois had a problem with shoplifting.

Alabama, in the 60s and early 70s, was a hotbed of racial conflict. Governor George Wallace had stood in the doors of the University of Alabama to prevent black students from enrolling. In Birmingham, the Ku Klux Klan had bombed the 16th street Baptist Church, killing four little girls. Some churches had made it plain that they did not want black members. Briarwood was not one of those churches.

Vernard Gant, a young African-American, became a Christian at the State Fair through Joyce Yancey, one of the women in our church. Our associate pastor, Ken Wilson, discipled him. After he finished high school, Briarwood helped him go to Columbia Bible College in Columbia, S.C. When he graduated, he came on our staff and helped us make an impact on the African-American community in Birmingham.

Vernard thought the best way to make an impact would be to ally Briarwood with an African-American church. We partnered with Sardis Baptist Church under the leadership of Dr. Sam Pettagrue. Sam is a very gifted man, and our churches built a close relationship.

We started a camping program for African-American

kids called Operation New Pace. A number of our members volunteered to serve on the committee that planned and staffed the camps.

One of the volunteers worked at the University of Alabama Medical Center. He told an African-American lady, Lois Coleman, who worked in his department, about our camping program. She was *very* skeptical about the genuiness of our motives. To check us out, she volunteered to help with the physicals we were giving several weeks before camp started.

The examinations took place at the church on Saturday morning. We had so many kids, the process took longer than we expected. When lunchtime came and we weren't finished, Howard Borland, who was part of our committee, said, "Bring all the kids to my home, and we'll feed them lunch."

We loaded up a hundred children and bussed them to his and Dixie's house, creating something of a youthful chaos.

"Why are you doing this?" Lois challenged Howard.

"The first reason is we love the Lord. And the second is we love these young people."

"No, you don't!" was her angry reply.

Howard patiently reassured her of his motives and then explained the gospel. Convinced of his sincerity, she committed her life to Christ and started attending Briarwood and my home Bible study. Six months later she began going through our membership class.

I hate to say it, but there were some people in our congregation who were opposed to black people seeking membership in the church. That had never been done in Birmingham. One of these men did some research on Lois and then called me.

"Frank, Lois Coleman isn't a Christian. She has been

arrested for shoplifting and has been in debtor's court on a number of occasions."

"I'll look into it," I told him and phoned Lois. "Is this true?" I asked after explaining the situation.

"Yes," she said, "I'm afraid so."

"Will you meet with our elders before they interview the membership class so they can ask you about this?"

"I'll be glad to," was her willing response.

The meeting was set up after Sunday night church. One of the elders asked, "When did you shoplift, before or after you became a Christian?"

"I shoplifted a number of times in 1970. Then in August, I became a Christian. In September, I shoplifted one more time and got caught. I had to spend the night in prison. I felt the Lord was saying to me, 'You're My child now. You stop that!' I told the women in prison that God was dealing with me, and we about had a revival!"

After one or two more questions, the elders asked her to wait outside while they discussed her situation. One of the men said, "I have to tell you that I have stolen before."

Another said, "If you had checked my credit, you never would have let me in this church!"

A third said, "The issue isn't what she has done, but whether she has truly repented and placed her faith in Christ."

All of them were convinced that she had and invited her back into the room. They told her she should meet with the class next Sunday. We wanted her to join the church with the class.

"Lois," I said, "you said you shoplifted a number of times in 1970 before you became a Christian. Did it occur to you to go back to those places and make restitution?"

She said, "No, it hadn't occurred to me."

"It's not a requirement for church membership. But it looks to me like it would be the right thing to do." I told her how I had paid back the $25 I had stolen.

When the church member who had researched Lois' background heard of our decision to accept her into church, he was angry. He wrote an inflammatory letter to everyone in the congregation. The letter arrived on Thursday, and I felt like I should answer it from the pulpit Sunday! However, there would be visitors in church who had not received the letter.

This was a real crisis.

Earlier in the year, I had selected the passages I would preach each Sunday. The Bible reference, Numbers 13-14, was already printed in the bulletin. We had started a series in Genesis the year before. We had marched through Exodus and Leviticus and now were in Numbers. Each week, I earnestly sought God's guidance on what to cover next.

I hadn't studied for the sermon yet because I had been busy counseling or doing church business. It took about ten hours to finalize my sermons, so most of my study had to be done at night.

When I began preparing, I realized that the passage answered the letter! God was not surprised. He knew this would happen and had directed me to that Scripture in advance. The passage was about the Israelites sending spies into the land God had promised to give them. Ten spies were convinced that if they tried to take the land, their children would be hurt. Two trusted God. They believed He would give them the land. The Israelites believed the ten and didn't trust God for protection of their children.

The inflammatory letter had said that if we proceeded with integration, our children would be hurt.

When the Israelites didn't obey the Lord, their children were hurt by having to live in the desert forty years longer until everyone who had been twenty years old at the start of the exodus died.

The letter also made other statements that the Scripture passage effectively answered. I never had to refer to the nasty letter when I preached on Sunday. But everyone who received it knew God had answered it.

Several weeks after Lois joined the church, she asked me, "Were you serious about my making restitution to those stores I stole from?"

"I think it would not only be the right thing, but you will feel that old burden lifted if you do."

"God must want me to do it because I can't get it off my mind. I want to repay them, but I'm afraid to go by myself. Will you go with me?"

"Sure, I will," delighted because I knew the Holy Spirit was working in her heart.

We agreed to go on a Saturday afternoon and drove to the first large mall in Birmingham. It was a ritzy place with nice shops. In the first store we asked to see the credit manager and were ushered into her office.

"I'm Frank Barker, pastor of Briarwood Presbyterian Church. This is Lois Coleman. She is a new Christian and a member of my congregation," I said. "Before she became a Christian, she shoplifted several times at your store. Now that she is a Christian, she would like to pay you back. She doesn't have any money, but she has a job. Would you set up a payment plan for her?"

The lady asked, "What did you shoplift?"

"I remember a $40 sweater, an $80 suit, a $60 dress, a $20 blouse and a $100 coat. I think that is all," Lois said.

Tears welled up in the credit manager's eyes. She said, "Wait a minute, please. I need to call the store manager!"

He came, and I went over everything again. He started crying, too. And I started passing out gospel tracts.

The next store was Blach's Department Store, and Lois owed them $400. Then we went to the largest department store in downtown Birmingham. Lois owed them $800. The manager there called the head of their security department.

He was dumbfounded. "I have been in the security business for thirty years. Only one other time someone sent an anonymous letter with some money. No one has ever come in person to pay back money like this before."

When we finished making the beginning of Lois' restitution she said, "I feel so clean!"

When she sent the money to Blach's they gave it to our church. Harold Blach was my friend in elementary school. Even though he is Jewish, he invited me to come to his store on Good Friday and give a devotional for his employees. I did it for the next ten years.

A few years later Lois was accepted on staff with Campus Crusade for Christ. After that, she went on staff with the Wales Goebel Ministry, reaching inner-city youth in Birmingham with the gospel.

She had always taken girls into her home who needed a safe place, but there were more than she could care for. She dreamed of a home where troubled youth or kids from dysfunctional families could learn about the Lord and have house-parents as role models. She inspired others with this dream and with the assistance of a board of interested people, she opened Grace House in 1992 with eight girls.

Plans are currently being made to buy property next to Grace House for more homes. A very capable executive director takes the everyday responsibilities off of Lois' shoulders so she can spend all her time ministering to the girls.

There were about seven families who did leave the church because we welcomed all of God's people no matter what color they happened to be. The group formed a little church, but it didn't last long. When their leader got cancer, I went to see him. He apologized and asked me to forgive him, which I was happy to do.

"Frank, will you preach at my funeral? I know I'm not going to be here long."

I think he realized heaven was not going to be racially divided. God created all men equal. In God's eyes, the only difference between black and white is whether or not we've trusted in Christ.

31

Street brawl

"Local Pastor Embroiled in Street Brawl." Only visions of the morning headlines kept me from jumping out of my car.

In the 1970s the radical ideas of the 60s not only continued, but were gaining a wider acceptance. The leaders of our country were setting a bad example to the youth of our nation by stealing and lying in the Watergate scandal. Children were sacrificed on the altar of selfishness when abortion was legalized in Roe v Wade.

I came out of the medical center after visiting one of our members who was sick. The cars in front of and in back of mine were so close, I had to inch forward and backward to get out of the parking place. After minutes of this jockeying, I looked back down the street so I could pull out. There were no cars coming. Only one was waiting at the red light half a block away. As I eased out into the street, there was a screech of brakes and a horn blasting like a semi-truck was about to crunch me flat.

I nearly jumped through the roof! When I calmed down and looked back, the car that had been at the red light was stopped at my bumper! Two guys in it were laughing their heads off at my reaction.

Obviously, they had seen me struggling to get out of the parking place. As soon as the light changed they flew to catch me, slammed on their brakes and sat on their horn.

That was *not* funny! Wrath, dark and filled with hatred, started at my ankles and flashed like a hot wave to the top of my head. I was furious! What's wrong with all these hippies. They're probably draft dodgers. I had an overwhelming desire to get out of my car, pull them out of theirs and beat them to a bloody pulp: that is, before they beat me up. To get in a couple of good licks would have been worth the beating.

Instead, I gripped the steering wheel and just sat there fuming in the middle of the street. Only visions of the next morning headlines, "Local Pastor Embroiled in Street Brawl," kept me from jumping out of my car.

I gave myself a lecture. *This overpowering rage is sin. God says I am to love my enemy, and bless those who curse me. I am to do good to those who spitefully use me. And here I am filled with anger and hatred. This is wrong. It doesn't matter what they did, my reaction is wrong! I've got to deal with this.*

"Lord," I prayed, "this is sin. I confess it. I repent of it. I ask you to take it out of my heart. I give up the right to be angry because you command me to love those men. I reject this anger." My hands relaxed on the steering wheel. Then I added, "I forgive them."

My ugly feelings had been so intense that I was amazed how my heart changed. The pressure lifted. The anger subsided. As calmness crept into my heart, I turned, waved and drove off. About a block away white hot anger again flashed over me. Those "hoods"! They're jerks! There is no respect for adults anymore! I can't believe they did that to me. I was furious! I really wanted to turn around and see if I could find them! The term "road rage" hadn't been coined yet, but that's what I felt.

Repeating the same process of confessing and asking the Lord's forgiveness kept rage from taking control of my mind. I had to confess and repent about ten times between the medical center and the church. Twenty minutes later, I pulled into the church parking lot feeling at peace with God and man.

I didn't do this in my own strength. I had to totally rely on the power of God's Spirit in me. It's funny how God teaches me to practice what I preach.

He taught me another lesson when I preached at the Jimmie Hale Mission. I prayed and asked the Father to fill and control me with the Holy Spirit. Then I added, "Lord, I am preaching at the Jimmie Hale Mission tonight. As proof that you really are filling me with the Holy Spirit, will you save eight of those men?"

The Mission is not in the best part of town. I drove down the Red Mountain Expressway, turned off on First Avenue and found a parking place under a street light near the front door. Homeless men, or bums as they were called before the term became politically incorrect, loitered on the sidewalk waiting for a free meal and bed for the night. Chapel services were held after dinner and that's when I would speak. The men were expected to attend.

Brother Leo Shepura ran the place. He met me at the door and greeted me with an enthusiastic handshake and smile that crinkled his face. He radiated joy and really loved the men at the mission. "Frank," he said, "I'm so glad you came to preach for us."

"I'm glad to be here," I said, and meant it. "Am I in time for supper?"

"Sure, we're just ready to eat," he said and opened the door to the dining room.

We all filed down the cafeteria line where the cooks filled our plates with good home-cooked food. The men ate like it was the only meal they had eaten that day. When everyone finished, Brother Leo announced, "Take your plates and glasses to the kitchen window before you leave. Chapel starts in ten minutes."

I followed Brother Leo down the hall into the large chapel room. The men ambled in and we all joined in singing hymns.

Brother Leo made a few announcements then introduced me. My heart was beating hard as I opened my Bible and launched into my sermon. I was expecting God to do great things. I preached the plan of salvation as clearly as I could and closed with an invitation for the men to give their hearts to the Lord and come forward to profess their decision.

A few days later I was talking to Elizabeth Newbold, a great Bible teacher and soul winner in Birmingham and later the world. I told her about asking God to fill me with the Holy Spirit and my prayer for confirmation. "Elizabeth, do you know how many men came forward to be saved?" I asked.

"Yes," she said and looked me dead in the eye. "Not a one! Frank, you have to accept the filling of the Holy Spirit by faith like the rest of us. Then you have to leave the results to God."

She nailed me.

"Oh, I see. I had been wanting God to prove that I was filled with the Spirit by having eight men trust Christ. I guess I hadn't really believed He had filled me."

"Exactly!" she said.

Now I was having to trust God to fill me with the Spirit to control my road rage. This is impossible to do in your own strength. It was like me trying to quit liking girls or change myself when I was just out of college. The more I tried to change myself, the more guilty and discouraged I became. But when I asked Christ to save me, God's Spirit came into my heart. He gave me His power to live the Christ-like life.

I had preached the Sunday before my road-rage incident, "If you must not repress, or suppress, or express anger, what do you do with it?" Then I explained our proper response. "We should confess our anger and really repent of it."

I found that knowing the right thing to do and doing it are two different things. But through God's Spirit in me, the newspaper didn't get the opportunity to report, "Local Pastor Embroiled in Street Brawl."

32

North and South

"Spank, smank!" my second daughter, Peggy, challenged me when she was a little girl. I can still see her arms akimbo, chin stuck out defiantly and little golden curls bobbing.

That was her attitude when I told all the kids I was going to spank them for disobeying their grandmother. They had lead her on a merry chase around the house as she had tried to get them in bed the night before.

Each of my kids was so different. It was hard to believe they all came from the same parents. Nita and Frank moaned at the prospect of a spanking, but not Peggy.

"Okay," I said. "I've changed my mind. I'm going to switch you." Peggy needed something stronger than a spanking. Barbara and I realized that if the children didn't submit their wills to us, they wouldn't submit to God. "Switch, smitch." Peggy said. She didn't stick out her tongue, but that was her attitude.

I walked into the yard and came back with a good switch. "Okay, Frank, you first. Pull up your pants legs." As I switched his little legs he jumped and cried as if I were chopping them off.

"Yikes! I'm getting out of here!" Peggy ran for the door, but I reached out and caught her. After her switching, we hugged, and she said she was sorry.

In 1962, prayer in public schools had been ruled unconstitutional by the Supreme Court. Two years later we started a Christian school at the church.

My kids attended the school from its beginning. They loved going to school at church, but I wondered if being the "preacher's kids" might add a little extra pressure on them.

We had planned to have K-4 and K-5 through first grade the first year, then add more grades each year. Because of the number of parents who wanted Christian schooling for their children, we went to six grades the second year. One teacher taught two grades. After that we added a grade a year till we had K through 12.

One of the hardest things about being the pastor and having final authority over the school was expelling kids. Some were children of solid church members, and I knew they wanted the influence of the Christian school for their children. Disagreements in the Session were another hard thing I had to deal with.

Back then, our Session was so small we met in my office. At one point our Session was divided over some aspects of our philosophy. It got so bad that all issues ended in a deadlock. I prayed and prayed for a solution. At our next meeting I said, "We have an irresolvable conflict. The solution is for Briarwood to help you Session members who have a different philosophy of ministry start a new church. We will buy land and help you build a church." It was something like Paul and Barnabas splitting over John Mark which ended in two good teams.

Thus, Faith Presbyterian Church was formed. Time has proven this to be the God-given solution. We began to move forward, and Faith Church is headed into their second building program.

Each year it seemed we needed to add another building for the school and the church. We built several buildings on our property including a gym and football field. Finally, our land and buildings were maxed out. We needed a new location for our growing school.

A couple in our church, Joe and Peggy Scotch, gave twenty acres of land seven miles south of our main location. We purchased an adjoining twenty acres and built a high school with a gym, lunchroom and football field.

Not only was our school outgrowing the old location, but our church was also bursting at the seams. Our sanctuary seated 900, but its two morning services were packed. We had overflow seating in the fellowship hall with the service "piped" in. Sunday school rooms and the nursery were overcrowded, and there was no space for new classes.

We asked part of the congregation to meet for a nine o'clock Sunday school and ten o'clock church service in our new high school gym. We called this new location, "Briarwood South." The other services were continued at "Briarwood North," the name we gave our main location.

Sundays, I preached at an 8 a.m. service at Briarwood North. Then I drove to Briarwood South and did a 10 a.m. service in the gym. I would then hurry back to the 11 a.m. service at the main location, arriving after the music was over at about 11:26. I did that for twelve years.

In 1976, I preached at a missions conference in Mississippi. I stayed in the home of Dr. Byrle and Mary Jo Kynerd. Byrle was teaching at a junior college there. We needed a new headmaster for our school. I was extremely impressed with the Kynerds and our school board offered Byrle the job. He accepted, and Mary Jo headed up the kindergarten.

Today, Briarwood Christian School has grown to approximately 1,750 students and 140 staff. It has excelled under Dr. Kynerd's leadership spiritually, academically and athletically. In 2002, 106 graduates ranked in the top four percent in the country on ACT scores.

Dr. Paul A. Kienel wrote, "As founder and now President Emeritus of the Association of Christian Schools International, it has been my privilege to visit hundreds of Christian schools around the world. It is my personal opinion that Briarwood Christian School is not only an exceptional school, but it is the foremost Christian school in the world today."

We also started a seminary at Briarwood. We saw a need for men and women to be trained for full-time Christian service. So Rev. Bill Hay, pastor of Covenant Presbyterian Church, and I founded Birmingham Theological Seminary in 1972.

Through the years, many people attended the seminary. During its twenty-seven year history, more than 2,500 students have taken one or more courses. Master's degrees have been awarded to 192 students, and there are now 29 faculty members. One of the students who came to seminary had a significant effect on my family.

Bob Barnes was the one who thought he was a Christian until I led the family he had visited to the Lord. Bob's family lived down the street from us at the time, but later moved to Montgomery. Several years later their grown son, Billy, moved back into their old home. Often he would stop by our house while jogging. I made a point of going out and talking to him. After a while I invited him to go with me to my Thursday night home Bible study.

The next Thursday, Billy picked me up to go to the study. As I was walking around his car to the passenger side, he quickly stuffed several beer cans under the seat. At a red light he stopped suddenly, and the cans rolled out. I didn't say anything, but just tucked them back under the seat.

A day or so later he phoned me at the church and said, "Mr. Barker, can you recommend a book on guilt?"

"Yes," I said.

"What's it called. I'll get it at the church bookstore."

"Come by my office, I've got it right here."

"Just tell me the name, I'll pick it up."

"It's okay, just come on over."

An hour later he walked into my office and asked, "What's the name of the book?"

I held up a Bible. I explained how, when Christ forgives our sin, our guilt is taken away. "I have a little booklet that my friend gave me when I was about your age. It's called 'What Does It Mean to Believe?'" I figured he was embarrassed about the beer cans and was under conviction.

Billy thanked me, took the Bible and went home and read the booklet over and over. He trusted Christ as his Savior and soon enrolled in our seminary. A few years later he came on our church staff and worked with the singles ministry at a two-thirds cut in salary. This is where our oldest daughter, Anita, was brought in contact with him after she graduated from college. But that's another story.

33

Staying on course

History in the making

As a pilot, I understood the value of staying on course. If I got off only one degree at the beginning of a cross-country flight, I would arrive hundreds of miles away from my proper destination. The same thing can happen with a church. If the church begins to slip in small ways from the truth of the Scripture, it also will get off course.

At the end of the 60s and early 70s the American churches, instead of influencing society for righteousness, began to accommodate the immorality of the times. Church leaders were picking and choosing what they wanted to believe in the Bible and saying the rest was not necessarily true. It became very popular to say, "Men wrote the Bible." They conveniently didn't believe the verse that says, "All Scripture is God breathed," or inspired by God.

Briarwood was part of the P.C.U.S. (Presbyterian Church of the United States) denomination. Its leaders were leaning more and more toward this "liberal" interpretation of the Scriptures. They were even trying to push us into joining the Presbyterian Church USA, which had departed from believing the whole truth of the Bible. If this merger took place, any influence of those who believed in the inerrancy of Scripture would be lost. There were several groups of concerned churchmen who were trying to counter this drift before it became a wholesale landslide into apostasy.

Delegates from these groups met in Atlanta late that year and wrote a Declaration of Commitment. 800 pastors signed this statement vowing commitment to the doctrine of the Westminster Confession of Faith, the Catechisms and historic Presbyterian policy.

I was one of the speakers at this rally in Atlanta called Presbyterian Churchmen United. The following are excerpts from my speech:

The road behind

"Let me try to give you a bird's-eye view of the road behind. Maybe it could best be described as a gradual curve, a decline from the standards of the truth of what the church has stood for.

"For example, we find a statement like this one from the adult study book, *Christian Doctrine*: 'You don't have to try to buy God's love and acceptance, because you are already loved and accepted by God, without any qualifications or prerequisites.' This statement is from page 317 of a book by one of my seminary professors. He is a Universalist. His statement is a dangerous half-truth. *Loved*, yes! *Accepted*, no! Not until we receive Christ as Savior.

"This same book states, 'Nor does it (the Bible) say that if man's sins are atoned for in one way or another, then God will forgive him.' This is a flat denial of our great need of atonement. The Bible does say, 'without shedding of blood there is no forgiveness of sin' (Hebrews 9:22). The Shorter Catechism states: 'Christ executeth the office of a priest in His once offering up of Himself a sacrifice to satisfy divine justice, and reconcile us to God...'

"The standards that are violated by the Presbytery are legion. Recently, a minister refused to affirm that Christ died for his sins. This man was accepted as a minister in Birmingham. In a Texas presbytery, a minister was passed who would not affirm belief in the resurrection of Christ.

"Such deviations from the standards of the Church are increasing. Our Church has been deviating from Presbyterianism. There are those who would say that this pattern *is* 'Presbyterianism,' but they are wrong.

"The Confession of Faith and the Larger and Shorter Catechism, '...are accepted by the Presbyterian Church in the United States as standard expositions of the teachings of Scripture in relation to both faith and practice' (Book of Church Order, p.102-1). When Christian education materials are not in accord, loyalty to our Presbyterian Church means *don't use them*.

"The road behind? A gradual curve away from the standards of our faith. The road ahead? What will it be like?"

A rough, unmarked road

"First, the road ahead will be *rough*. How could it be otherwise? As Calvin wrote: 'A dog barks when his master is attacked. I would be a coward if I saw that God's truth is being attacked and yet would remain silent.' We must not shrink from standing for God's truth.

"'Excessive aversion to controversy,' said James Stalker, 'may be an indication that a church has no keen sense of possessing truth which is of any great worth, and that it has lost appreciation for the infinite difference in value between truth and error.'

"Second, the road ahead is *uncharted*. No one can predict exactly what is going to happen. There are too many variables. There would seem to be two ultimate possibilities in this present conflict. We have drawn the battle line at certain crucial issues which are outlined in our Declaration. Either we win or we lose in those issues, and we should prepare ourselves and our people for either eventuality."

Win or lose - no draw

"If we win, we must press our advantage. We must not be satisfied only to win on the issues where we've drawn the battle line. The conditions that produced the issues must be changed. We must go for the disease, not just the symptoms. We must have as our goal to return the program of our Church to alignment with the standards of truth. Personnel must be changed in our boards and agencies and in our seminaries.

"If we lose, we must be prepared. If we compromise at any of the major points outlined in the Declaration, we are in effect veering from Presbyterianism or, more important, from biblical Christianity!

"We are moving to a situation in which a minister is not required to hold to basic Christian beliefs. This is unscriptural."

Purity and peace

"In the *Book of Church Order*, we are told that 'Christ, as King and Head of the Church ... has ordained His system of ... government ... insofar as this system is expressly set forth in Scripture, nothing may be added or taken away' (*Book of Church Order*, p.27, 6, 7).

"In other words, we said that we believed the basic form of government we practice is laid down in Scripture, and we aren't free to change it. We defend our basic teachings at all costs. Such were the vows many of us have taken.

"A departure from our vows would cost us spiritual power. I believe that compromise on these points will cause the Spirit of God to withdraw His blessing. He is the Spirit of truth and will bless only the truth."

Straight and narrow

"Rather than take a turn which would eliminate the requirement that ministers must hold certain beliefs, many will continue straight ahead. This is the third point: There may well be a fork in the road. But if so, it will not be we who are departing; we will continue straight on. We invite men from all the nation to join us, if and when that time comes.

"If the Christian education program of our denomination is wanting, that is not reason for our local church's program to suffer. There is top-notch material available from other sources.

"The same is true in the area of evangelism. It is time to quit wringing our hands over the lack of materials and begin warming our hearts with the materials and training offered by other groups. It is time to quit throwing our hands in the air over ineffective denomination programs and begin throwing our weight behind effective programs of outreach wherever they are found.

"Above all, we must really set our people to praying! Weekly prayer groups should be organized. I challenge you: invite men to weekly prayer breakfasts at your home and everybody pray!

"We have suggested that the road ahead will be rough, that it is uncharted and may lead to a fork. One final and all-important point: the road ahead has a guide. God has promised to guide His people. He says: 'Trust in the Lord with all your heart and don't lean on your own understanding. In all your ways acknowledge Him, and He will direct your paths' (Prov. 3:5-6).

"I believe that if we put our trust in God and earnestly pray, He will guide each step along this rough and uncharted road ahead. But note the further condition:

we must acknowledge Him in all our ways. It will not do for us to affirm God's truth ever so loudly on other issues if we flinch on these we have outlined.

"As Luther said: 'If I profess with the loudest voice and clearest exposition every portion of the truth of God except precisely that little point which the world and the devil are at the moment attacking, I am not confessing Christ, however boldly I may be professing Christ. Where the battle rages, there the loyalty of the soldier is proved, and to be steady on all the battlefield besides, is merely flight and disgrace if he flinches at that point.'"

Withdrawal

When I left the meeting in Atlanta, I wanted to inform my people at Briarwood about what was going on in the denomination. The "fear of the sneer or the leer of the peer," as Bud Newbold always says, is what shuts the mouths of many Christians. When respected leaders are claiming a "higher interpretation," it makes it even more difficult to stand up and say they are wrong. However, the gospel must be guarded and kept pure. So I communicated to my congregation the following points and issues:

"It is difficult to protect the flock," I said. "If I were to leave Briarwood, it would be difficult to get another like-minded minister. A church in New Orleans lost their pastor, and the Presbytery there would not allow them to call a conservative man. They held out for eight years, and the church was about to go under before they received permission to call a Bible-believing minister.

"The situation in the Presbyterian Church U.S. is seen in a pastoral letter written by the Moderator of the General Assembly. He wrote, "We have to learn to live with diversity." The problem is that what he called "diversity" God calls APOSTASY! It is pure heresy! It is not diversity when a college professor in one of our denomination's colleges writes a book, *Was Jesus Married?*, and denies the virgin birth. It is not diversity when a minister in our Presbytery refuses to affirm that Christ died for his sins! It is not diversity when a woman was ordained to the pastorate even though she made a clear statement of believing in Universalism. It is apostasy!

"For thirteen years, those like minded with me have lived with this. When we oppose or protest these heresies, we're the ones who get disciplined!

"Francis Schaeffer wrote, 'When a church comes to the place where it can no longer exert discipline, then with tears before the Lord, we must consider a second step. If the battle for doctrinal purity is lost, we must understand that there is a second step to take in regard to the practice of the principle of purity of the visible church. It may be necessary for true Christians to leave the visible organization with which they have been associated. But note well: If we must leave our church, it should always be with tears... We are not practicing separation... The Bible's principle of the practice of purity of the visible church is a positive concept' (*The Church Before the Watching World*).

"Our denomination did many things which caused me to weep and in which I felt involved in the guilt. The most abhorrent to me was in the matter of the official endorsement of abortion for socio-economic reasons. In 1971-72, our denomination spent $92,166.65 to secure abortions for 341 persons! **Abortion is murder**! We could not justify remaining in a body that advocates and actually participates in murder!

"Truth must come before tradition or institutions. The Church must be judged by the Word of Truth. 'The invisible Church is more important than the visible church, and loyalty to the former may involve either expulsion or separation from the latter, and the formation of a new visible church.' (*The Basis of Christian Unity*, D. Martyn Lloyd-Jones).

It was not long after this that the Session called a congregational meeting following the II a.m. service on May 6, 1973. I read the resolution the Session adopted. The church voted to withdraw from the PCUS. I closed in prayer asking God to guide us and that we would be united in heart and spirit and love.

There was unity in our church and unanimous agreement with the Session's resolution of withdrawal. The congregation at Briarwood withdrew from the PCUS on September 30,1973.

A new denomination

During the period from February, 1973, up to the time of the first General Assembly in December, the new denomination was called The Continuing Presbyterian Church. The first General Assembly met at Briarwood on December 4, and the denomination name was changed to National Presbyterian Church. But due to a name conflict with the National Presbyterian Church of Washington, D.C., the name was changed again the next year to The Presbyterian Church of America (PCA).

The Birmingham Presbytery (PCUS) had purchased ten acres of land for $25,000 where we built Briarwood. In our settlement agreement for withdrawal, they asked us to buy them ten acres, which we did. In ten years land prices had escalated beyond anyone's imagination.

We paid $50,000 for ten acres a half mile from our church. The PCUSA never built on that land, but later sold it for $85,000.

It was amazing to be a part of this historic event. Because a number of men and women stood on the truth and authority of God's Word, the PCA denomination was formed. In the past thirty years, this denomination has been a beacon shining the truth of God to a nation stumbling through the darkness of this age.

34

The ground beneath your feet

"Me! Me! Me!" The 1980s was a generation of status seekers. "If you've got it, flaunt it," or "You can have it all!," were the watchwords of our nation. The baby boomers were dubbed the "splurge generation." Video games, aerobics, mini-vans, camcorders and Oprah became part of our lives.

I knew by personal experience that all those things didn't bring true happiness. Things might make you happy for a little while, but they wear out or break down. Then you are looking for the next high. It made me all the more passionate to get the truth to people. Jesus Christ sets you free. In Him, you are free indeed.

By the mid 80s, the church had grown so much that I needed someone else to take over our evangelism program. However, I wanted to continue my involvement as a trainer and partner with first-timers. When they learned the gospel presentation, I had them share with people we called on. I don't know which is more fun, seeing someone come to the Lord with me or watching my trainee lead someone into the kingdom.

We hired an outstanding young man, Rev. Ron Steel, to head up our Outreach Department. When he came on board I said, "Dr. James Kennedy at Coral Ridge Presbyterian has developed a program called Evangelism Explosion. Why don't you go down there and check it out."

Ron spent a week observing the E.E. program and came home so enthusiastic that we decided to shift our training to their model. It was a lot like my long presentation, but had some material and concepts which mine lacked. The E.E. program had "training cycles" that we built into our training manual. It worked on a sixteen-week cycle.

It was basic "ground school," with 30 to 40 minutes of class time and then they'd team up for "in-flight training." The teams called on newcomers to Birmingham or people who had visited Briarwood. Those who showed interest in the gospel were invited to a pot-luck dinner held in a church member's home. Usually, we had a husband and wife share their testimony, then I concluded the program by giving a "capsule form" of the gospel. I encouraged those who had questions to talk to me about their salvation and growth in Christ.

Coral Ridge Church continued to refine their E.E. training, and we adopted it as our main method for outreach. One of their staff came and taught those experienced in evangelism to be trainers. In September of that year we started the first semester of E.E. with twenty-five trainers and fifty trainees. Every trainer recruited a prayer team to pray for their trainees and visits.

We soon needed a full-time director and secretary for the Outreach Department. Mark Roessler came on board and managed and developed new approaches to church growth. He also aided other departments of the church in evangelistic outreaches.

You don't have to go to Africa to be a missionary. Your mission field is the ground between your own two feet.

35

Cream of wheat again!

"What do you think?" Barbara and I stood in front of our children in the living room. They were old enough now and we thought their opinion must be considered.

Anita was eighteen and heading to that great southern school Auburn University, my alma mater. (Of course, I'm not biased.) Barbara came to me concerned that Anita wouldn't be able to be involved in some of the college activities because our level of giving was maxed out.

"We cannot impose our way of life on our children. We have to discuss it with them," she said.

"All right," I agreed. "Let's get them together and ask their opinion."

When everyone had gathered, I said, "Frank, Anita, Peggy, up to this point your mother and I have made the decision about how much of our family income to give to the Lord. But now you are starting to go off to college, and the decision will affect what activities you can enter into. So we believe you should have a part in making the decision. We are wrestling with whether we should back off some in our giving. Things have been very tight financially this year. Your mom and I would like you to pray about how much of our salary we should give." At this point we were giving 75 percent of our salary back to the Lord.

After a time of praying together, young Frank III settled the issue. He said, "God has never let us down. I don't think we should step back from our present level of giving."

Nita, who loves pretty things and enjoys going out with her friends and to her grandmother's country club, was also in agreement with Frank. "I don't either. I believe we should continue to give to the Lord at our present level. However, I don't think we should increase it again this year."

Peggy also believed we were following God's will.

They remembered the time their mother had awoken them and shown them the $600 that God had provided for our bills. They remembered how God had always given us just what we needed when we needed it. They had seen the missionaries receive exactly the money they needed. Seeing God's provision as they were growing up had given them a love and trust for Him that made them want to continue our way of giving.

Barbara remembered the early years of learning to trust the Lord with our finances. After coming from an affluent home, it was difficult at first to have to wait on the Lord.

Several years before, when the children were little, I went to Korea to preach. Before I left, Barbara looked at me and said, "What am I going to feed the children? I have only $15 to last the rest of the month."

It was so hard for me to leave her. I took her in my arms and hugged her tightly. "Pray, Honey. God will provide. I know He will."

In a small voice she answered into my shoulder, "Pray with me before you leave. I feel better about praying when you're here."

I did pray and she was comforted, but it still didn't make it easy for either one of us. I got on the plane with a suitcase full of antacids. Not until I returned home did I learn how bad things were for her, but also how God met her needs.

The money and groceries did give out. The only thing in the house to feed the children was cream of wheat.

They ate it for supper four days in a row. On the third day of cream of wheat, a friend called.

"Barbara!" she exclaimed. "You'll never believe what I just bought. I'm coming by to show you."

Half an hour later her friend pulled into our driveway. She showed her the new dress she bought. "It was a $150 dress, but I only paid $39 for it. Can you believe it! Isn't it gorgeous?"

Barbara forced a smile. "Oh, it's so pretty, and you will look so cute in it." Inside, she seethed against me and God. Her friend didn't need that dress. She only got it because it was on sale. *And my children and I are eating cream of wheat AGAIN!* she thought.

Barbara remembered to fake it. "I love it!"

Another friend called later that same day and asked, "I'm going to the store for groceries. Do you need anything?"

"YES!" Barbara wanted to scream. "I need a lot of things, but I can't tell you about it." What actually came out of her mouth, with her good southern training, was, "No, thank you. We're doing fine."

When she hung up the phone she raged. *This is wrong! We can't make our children live this way!*

Peggy came in as Barbara was standing over the stove, "Mom, what's for dinner?"

"Cream of wheat," Barbara answered not looking up as she stirred the vile white goo. She thought to herself, *Frank and I are voluntarily putting the children through something they don't have to go through!*

Much to Barbara's surprise, Peggy cheered, "All right! No peas and carrots!" She rushed out of the kitchen shouting the "good news" to Nita and Frank III.

Suddenly, it was like the Wise Men's star shone its light into the little kitchen. She saw everything in a new and different way. She looked at the clean water that was pouring out of the faucet as she rinsed off her hands. The electric stove was cooking the "supper" and her china gleamed in the cabinet.

Glancing in the den she saw all three children lying on the floor doing their homework and chatting happily. All of them loved the Lord and were walking with Him. They were all strong and healthy.

She looked around the house at all the beautiful furnishings God had provided for their home.

I have a level of 'have-to-have,' she thought. *My gratitude begins just **above** that.* It was like God said to her, "Look around you. See what you have to be grateful for." She began to give thanks to the Lord for everything she saw.

The next morning a friend called, "Barbara, I've been trying to get over to your house for days. Are you going to be home? I have a check to give you."

Barbara had learned to be thankful in all things, and I had not backed away from my pledge to God. I was still amazed and grateful that He had saved me. God had given me true freedom. It was a joy to give back to Him.

Because of our giving, our children have carried on their trust in God and their desire to give Him their time, talents and treasures also. Even now they continue what they learned in our home with their own families.

Take the initiative

"Well, hell froze over today," a former member said when he walked into my office.

"Oh?" was all I could think of to say.

"Yes," he replied, "I had vowed that before I'd set foot in this church again, hell would freeze over!"

This reconciliation was the result of a sermon I preached on Matthew 5:23-24. "If you are offering your gift at the altar and there remember that your brother has something against you, leave your gift there in front of the altar. First go and be reconciled to your brother; then come and offer your gift."

A few days after I preached, the audio manager said, "We've lost the tape of last Sunday's sermon. Would you mind preaching it again in a sound booth so I can tape it?"

"Didn't they sell some tapes in the bookstore?" I asked. "Advertise in our newsletter and maybe someone will return one."

Nobody turned one in, so the sound manager set me up with a tape recorder, and I preached that sermon to myself. When I finished, he went to get the tape.

"Uh oh!" He grinned sheepishly at me. "This thing quit recording shortly after you got started. I don't understand it. I've never had any trouble with this recorder before. Would you mind doing it again?"

This was weird. I prayed, "Lord, are you trying to tell me there is someone I need to be reconciled with? If so, please show me."

Through the years God had used different ways to

guide me. Here again was one of the "stars" He used to point the way He wanted me to go. It "so happened" that an individual in the church came to my office the next week and said, "I believe you need reconciliation with that former member who withdrew from the church."

He didn't have to draw me a picture. The face of a Sunday school teacher who was seriously off in some doctrinal areas flashed into my mind. The man was a gifted teacher in the sense that he presented his lesson well, but he would not listen to any correction. Finally, the chairman of the Christian Education Committee came to me and said, "We've got to do something!"

This teacher had a following in the church; and if we just removed him from teaching, it could damage the church body. The elders decided to ask all the teachers to sign a doctrinal statement that they would not knowingly teach anything contrary to our denomination's doctrinal standards. He wouldn't sign, and his family left the church. At least it didn't cause division.

I realized the Lord had been speaking to me through that passage of Scripture I had preached on three times now. I got the message loud and clear. The next Saturday afternoon I went to his home; and the minute I rang the door bell, he opened the door. He was all smiles and invited me in.

"Jim told me that you have something against me, and I wanted to come try to make matters right and ask your forgiveness."

He said, "I knew God answered prayer, but I didn't know He did it so immediately. I've been in a spiritual tailspin for two years. This morning I got down on my knees in this very room and asked God to do something to help me get this bitterness out of my heart, and this afternoon you came!"

"I've been trying to come for several days," I confessed, "but things kept coming up."

"If you had come before today, I wouldn't have let you in the house," he said with a big grin.

We worked our way through the issues. He had gotten the idea that once we had him out of teaching, we quit asking our teachers to sign that statement.

"Oh, no," I told him. "You were the occasion for our initiating that procedure, but it is something we should have been doing all along, and we plan to keep doing it."

We were reconciled and his bitterness was healed, but he didn't plan on coming back to Briarwood. So I was surprised when he walked into my office a week later and said, "Well, hell froze over today." The big grin on his face spoke volumes.

"Oh? It did?" was all I could think of to say.

"Yes," he replied, "I had vowed that before I'd set foot in this church again, hell would freeze over!" We both laughed. Then he said, "It meant so much to me for you to come see me. I believe there is someone else you need to go see." He told me it was a lady who had left our church because we didn't let her teach.

"I have already called her and urged her to come back. She told me that the reason she wouldn't come back was that she knew a lot more about the Bible than a number of teachers, but we wouldn't let her teach. I told her there were requirements for teaching in addition to knowledge. She quizzed me with a 'Like what?' And I began, 'For one thing, teachers need to be loving and...' She cut me off with a growl, 'I'M LOVING!' I don't think she is ready to come back."

Everything doesn't always "work out" the way we think it should. But I have learned I am not responsible for the way other people act. However, I am responsible for the way I act. I need to take the initiative to do what's right in the power of the Holy Spirit. Then I leave the results of how others respond to God.

Learning to love people you don't like is a hard lesson to learn. Dr. Billy Kim, a pastor from Korea and the director for the Far Eastern Broadcasting Company, was speaking at a luncheon from I Corinthians, chapter 13. Dr. Kim challenged us to take someone we didn't like and start treating them with the I Corinthians 13 kind of love.

I decided to try it on a minister in our Presbytery I didn't care for. He didn't much like me either. I thought he was too narrow in his views, and I'm sure he thought me too broad.

We didn't have much contact because he pastored in Anniston, which is about an hour away from Birmingham. Every four months we saw each other at Presbytery meetings. I began to pray for him and asked God to help me love him with the love of God.

It happened to be his turn to preach at the next meeting of the Presbytery. I made it a point to tell him I thought he did an excellent job. He was shocked. A few months later, he called and asked me to come do a sermon series at his church. I gladly accepted, and the conference went well.

Not long after that, he and his officers had a disagreement, and he resigned. He moved to Birmingham to sell insurance, which isn't much different from what a pastor does anyway: just a different kind of insurance. He and his family began attending Briarwood. We asked him to teach an adult Sunday school class, and he enrolled his children in our school.

After several years the PCA church in Tuscumbia, Alabama, was looking for a pastor, and I recommended him. He asked me to preach his installation sermon.

After several years he said, "You know, being at

Briarwood Church and school meant so much to our family. If you ever have a staff opening where I would fit, I would love to be considered."

About a year later we had an opening, and the search committee recommended him to head up our Christian Education Department. So George and Nancy Mitchell came to be part of our team and blessed us for several years.

My experience with George gave me a new appreciation for the way God can break down barriers between people. Through the power of the Holy Spirit, we can love by faith using I Corinthians 13 as a compass. What a difference this would make in our families, churches and businesses if people only realized the great power of God to love the people we don't like. If the Spirit of God can raise the dead, think what the Spirit of God can do in your life!

37

Eternal visions

"No Room for You." I thought this was how visitors felt when they tried to come to church on Sunday. By the mid 80s all three services were overflowing. People had to come very early just to get a parking spot.

No land was available around our main location on Highway 280 for us to build on. Large homes had been built on all sides of the church. A committee was appointed to study the issue. They recommended that we relocate. We had to move.

The committee looked for property not too far from our church. There wasn't much on the market. They found a large estate with sixty acres of land right off Interstate 459. It had one very nice home and a smaller one and was only three miles from our present site. We purchased the acreage and the houses for $3 million.

We had to sell the church on Highway 280 before we could move forward. A Bible college located near downtown Birmingham had outgrown its campus. Because we had a large elementary school with several buildings including a gym, our church was a perfect new campus for Southeastern Bible College.

What we should do with the part of the congregation at Briarwood South that didn't want to move to the new church remained an issue in need of prayer. We solved the problem by hiring Bob Flayhart to start a separate church at Briarwood South. A good solid core of our congregation that met at South stayed to help Bob Flayhart get the new church started. They named it Oak Mountain Presbyterian. It grew rapidly and now has its own facilities and school.

Our building committee was made up of men who had worked over the years with the Presbytery to plant new churches. They had the needed experience and worked hard on plans for the church and elementary school.

I got curious about how much the new buildings would cost and asked, "How much are you estimating it will cost to build what we need?"

The chairman said, "Maybe $10 million."

"What!" I was shocked. "I would never have considered moving if I had known that. Don't breathe a word of this outside this room! It couldn't cost that much!"

To raise the money we started the process of a Capital Funds Campaign and asked our people for a three-year commitment. From the pulpit I made the famous statement, "I believe we can have our new facility paid for when we move in." We could have done it if the cost had remained at $10 million. But then word came that our cost was going to be $13 million, then $17 million and then $20 million! When the bids actually came in, the cost, including the land, was $32 million! The congregation and the whole church staff were overwhelmed.

I was sick at heart. How could we spend that much money on buildings when there was so much need in the mission fields? But, the planners convinced me that building the school and having a church big enough for our 2,800 members would require that amount of money. We had to move ahead with our plans, not only because we needed more room for the congregation, but also because we had already sold our property. Plus, the clearing of the new property was in full swing.

I prayed, "Lord, what went wrong?" It wasn't the committee's fault. They had done a great job. Our architect's reputation for correct estimates on cost factors was the best. God knew our hearts. We weren't doing this for any reason other than removing barriers to growth.

As I prayed over what seemed like a big mistake, I realized nothing had gone wrong. The committee had done their job well and so had the architect. The buildings they had planned were what we believed God wanted us to build. He had prevented us from knowing the final cost because we never would have tackled it if we had. My heart was calmed and I knew God would enable us to meet the payments without cutting back on our giving to world or home missions.

I shared my thought with the congregation and God quieted their hearts, too.

The new property was on a hill. When the bulldozers started pushing dirt around preparing the site for construction there was a knee-deep muddy mess covering the hill. Rains washed it down the hill, across the street and into the yards and patios of the homes in the area. This wasn't the way to build good relationships with our new neighbors!

One Sunday evening after a big rain, a very irate group burst in the front door of our church. They were on their way to the pulpit to chastise the congregation! Fortunately, services had not started and I "just happened" to walk through the foyer when they came in. I calmed them down and promised I would personally see to it that all the mud was cleaned up.

The next day, several men and I took equipment out there and knocked on doors to tell the neighbors we were there to clean up the trash and mud on their property. One of our own members lived on the street and was so mad he threatened to sue the church!

After cleaning up, we promised that we would put up barriers so it wouldn't happen again. We also asked our members not to enter church property from that street in order to keep heavy traffic from annoying the neighbors. Peace was restored.

To raise the money we used successive three-year Capital Fund Campaigns that we termed "Briarwood Vision I, II, III, IV, and V." One of our members remarked, "I've heard of eternal life, but I didn't know about the 'Eternal Visions!'"

Actually, the challenge and need to give sacrificially moved our people significantly into deeper walks with God. Dr. Evan Zeiger, a neurosurgeon, had always wanted a Mercedes. Finally, he bought one. On his way home after work he stopped at a red light and closed his eyes to ask God what he could sacrifice for the current Vision Campaign. When he opened his eyes he was looking at the steering wheel of his new car. "Oh, no!" he thought. "Not my Mercedes!" By the time he arrived home, he had relinquished his prized car to the Lord. He shared his decision with his wife, Peggy. Later, he heard her crying.

"What's the matter?" he asked.

"You've really gotten into the spirit of this Vision giving," she said. "So, I asked the Lord what He wanted me to give. I believe He wants me to give my engagement ring."

To appreciate her sacrifice, you need to know the history of her ring. When she was a young lady, she saw a ring she really liked. She prayed, "God, this is the type of ring I want my husband-to-be to offer me when he proposes. That's how I'll know he's the one I am to marry."

Some time later, totally unaware of her prayer, Evan proposed to her with *that exact* ring!

I asked them to share their story with the congregation, and God used it to move many to new depths of sacrifice. Some friends of theirs, without their knowing it, bought the ring from the church and gave it back to her on their anniversary several years later.

Evan went without a car for many months and every day, rain or shine, he jogged to work. His office was five miles across town from their home.

There were many more outstanding stories I could tell about the sacrifices people made. Even children wanted to give what they had to help.

The Lord enabled us to pay the $32 million. A few years later we had to add additional facilities, which I never imagined we would ever need. They have also been paid for!

When we moved into our new church in January of 1988, Barbara and I looked at the beautiful new buildings and she remembered my prayer from the storefront days. I had asked God to make us a mighty church to reach the world for Jesus. She had thought, "Oh, bless his heart. How can our little church ever be *anything* that would impact the world?"

Forty years later, we both realized how exceedingly great God had answered that prayer. It certainly was not by my might or power that it was done. God's Spirit deserved and received all the credit.

The awesome power of God overwhelmed us as we looked at the magnificent new buildings that would house our congregation of 4,000, plus the many "regular visitors" who came to the church. Our church has 105 different ministries reaching the inner city and all parts of the globe. Oh, how God has heard our prayers and blessed us.

The large house on our property was decorated by some interior designers in the church. It is used for housing visiting speakers, Sunday school classes, small weddings, receptions, Bible classes, etc. The smaller house is used for counseling offices and Sunday school classes.

We all were delighted to be in our new buildings that were so large it took awhile to learn our way around. The worship center was not completed when we moved in, so we had to hold two services in the gym. The building committee would not let anyone in the worship center until it was completed so everyone could see its magnificence together.

The Sunday night of our first service in it, the chairman of the committee opened the service with the words from Psalms 122, "I was *glad* when they said unto me, 'Let us go into the house of the LORD.' Joy is the only word that described our feelings.

38

20/20 hindsight

"I wouldn't take a baby and make it crawl across the highway. First I'd teach it to walk, then run, then we'd work up to crossing the street. I'm afraid you aren't strong enough to do this," I told Peggy, our youngest daughter.

At age thirteen, Peggy wanted to study theater at the University of Montevallo for the summer. I would have preferred that she go to Africa as a missionary rather than study "fine arts." I did not want her to be exposed to some of the nasty plays and topics that would be required reading. Also, some college theater majors lived a lifestyle I didn't want Peggy exposed to at age thirteen.

We went round and round about it. I finally agreed to pray with her that if God wanted her to go, He would have to provide three things. God had always guided me, and I knew He would show us His will in this situation too.

One: Peggy would have to be accepted to study at the University at age thirteen.

Two: She would have to get a ride to and from the school every day. It was about a forty-five minute drive from our house to Montevallo.

Three: She would have to have a Christian adult to meet her during class breaks. I wanted her to be able to meet with someone Barbara and I trusted when she wasn't in class.

Peggy agreed to my stipulations and prayed earnestly. She was accepted as a student, and she marked number one off my list of conditions.

Twin girls who lived down the street from us had just received scholarships to Montevallo. They had the same schedule as Peggy and were looking for someone to car pool with them and help pay for gas. Number two down.

A girl Barbara had discipled for several years had moved to the town of Montevallo and taught at the University. When Peggy visited the campus, she saw her. This teacher told us, "I would love to have Peggy come to me on her class breaks."

I saw that God had provided answers for the three conditions I made. As much as I hated it, I let her study theater that summer. Acting was very important to Peggy, and I knew God had given her the talent and desire to pursue it. But I told her, "As much time as you spend reading these ungodly works, I want you to spend equal time in God's Word."

Peggy and I began memorizing Scripture and having our "quiet times" together. I knew it was hard on her, spending so much time with some of the amoral people involved in the drama department. I could see she was being stretched spiritually. She learned to make hard decisions that were unpopular with her peers, but right in God's eyes.

Like her mother, Peggy loved to talk. I needed to spend time with her asking questions and listening. When she was in high school, I would check her out of school and take her to lunch every now and then. Most of the time I'd only have a few dollars, so we'd split a bowl of French onion soup and have a good talk.

I made it a priority to be at every one of her opening performances because this was important to her. I'd get people to fill in for Bible studies or seminary classes I was teaching. My rule was to never be out of town on opening nights.

Every Christmas Peggy would write a Christmas drama as a gift for me. They were powerful stories that brought Scripture to life. I asked her to perform them for the PCA pastors in our December meetings.

One Christmas Eve, Peggy put a napkin over her head and spontaneously acted out her interpretation of what Mary said and thought when Jesus was born. The next morning was Sunday, and we had one large service instead of our usual two. As I looked out at almost 3,000 people who had gathered to worship the Lord on Christmas morning, the thought of Peggy playing Mary kept coming to my mind. I looked down from the pulpit and saw her smiling up at me.

"Peggy," I asked, "would you come up here and do for the congregation what you did for our family last night?" I surprised her socks off, but never before have I seen her so eloquent as that morning when she re-enacted her drama about Mary.

The Lord really used Peggy's theater training in my life as well as hers. Often as I prepared sermons the thought would come to me, *this would be wonderful as a drama.* I would take my sermon to Peggy, and she would write a skit and perform it for the church service. The drama would illustrate the exact point I wanted to make. It made the Scripture come to life. I was glad Peggy stayed in Birmingham for college, going to Samford University on a math/drama scholarship.

About the time Peggy started college, a young couple moved to Birmingham and came to Briarwood. The husband came to me for counseling because his wife wanted to leave him. This young man's name was Tim Townes. When his wife did leave, he and I became very close friends. He prayed with me in our early morning prayer group and came to my Bible study. We often met for lunch and counseling. Tim was a truly brilliant professor working in genetic biochemistry at the University of Alabama in Birmingham. Barbara and I grew to love and enjoy him very much.

Peggy moved out of the dorm her senior year and back home. She helped Barbara cook for the Saturday morning prayer breakfasts. Tim met her and asked for my permission to take her out for dinner. Less than a year later, he came to my office and asked for my permission again. This time it was to marry Peggy.

I was exhausted from being up late many nights in a row that week and wasn't thinking clearly. I said, "I'll ask Peggy if she wants to marry you. It's all right with Barbara and me."

I changed the subject and asked Tim about his work. The next thing I knew, I woke with a start to find that I had actually fallen asleep while listening to my future son-in-law! Tim told me later that he thought, *I would like to ask Peggy myself!*

Tim and Peggy were one of the last couples to be married in Briarwood's old sanctuary before the new church was built. Tim's two daughters by his first marriage were four and seven when they were married, and Peggy loved her stepdaughters. Barbara and I enjoyed them too. When they were in high school, they read Tim LaHaye's *Left Behind* books, and had a lot of questions about the end times. They asked me if I would help them with the things they didn't understand. I was thankful the girls felt comfortable enough with me to ask me to answer their questions. Peggy and Tim had four more children: Gil, Margaret Anne, David and Neely.

Peggy was not our only child faced with a life decision at an early age. When our oldest daughter Anita was in college at Auburn, she wanted to try out for the cheerleading squad. The night before the tryouts, she received a disturbing phone call.

"We're praying you won't make cheerleader," a couple of seniors told her.

Nita was stunned. "Why don't you want me to be a cheerleader?"

"Because its not the kind of atmosphere Christians should put themselves in. You have to say cuss words in the cheers, and you'll be around people who will have a bad influence on you."

Anita called me distraught with questions. Were these people right? Should she not try out for cheerleader? Is it really not the kind of position a Christian should be in?

After Anita graduated from high school, she worked for a cheerleading company. I had seen the choices she made in this environment. At that time, she knew of no other Christians working in cheerleading and was exposed to many bad influences. Her work in that environment changed her faith from being based on what Barbara and I believed to a personal faith of her own. I saw her make choices that were not popular, but honorable. She made a strong stand for Christ then, and I knew she would do the same at Auburn.

"Anita," I told her, "there's one thing I've learned."

"What's that, Daddy?"

"You cannot please everybody. There's always going to be somebody who doesn't like what you're doing and will try to put you down. You have to decide if this is what the Lord wants you to do. Are you doing this for *your* glory, or are you trying to bring glory and honor to Him?"

Barbara and I loved to watch our beautiful, tiny daughter get tossed in the air and shout "War Eagle!" during the games. She did have many opportunities to be a light shining in the darkness as an Auburn cheerleader. She learned how she could be "in the world but not of it." There were many chances to compromise, but she stood strong and had many opportunities to share her faith in Jesus.

After graduating from Auburn, Anita came back to Briarwood and worked with Stampede, our high school ministry. One day she came into my office and put her arms around my neck and said, "Daddy, I love you so much and want to marry someone just like you. When *you* find the man you think I should marry, will you let me know?"

In 1960, when I was going through the neighborhoods surveying people about starting a new church, I met Bob Barnes. He was mowing his lawn and stopped to talk to me. He turned off the mower and said he was interested in coming to the new church I was starting in the shopping center. He and his family did come and joined the church. When Barbara and I got married, he was on the committee to find us a house. He chose one down the street from him with the same floor plan as his house. They moved to Montgomery, but many years later his son Billy came back to Birmingham and lived in their old house. He's the one who asked for a book on guilt and became a Christian. He was very sharp and became the head of Briarwood's singles' ministry. I really enjoyed him. He also attended my prayer group and Bible study.

I suggested he ask Anita to a banquet our Bible study group was having, so he called her.

"Oh," she said, "I'm sorry I can't go, I already have another date that night."

"Oh really? When is your date?" he asked.

"I'm going out at 8:00," she said.

"Me too! But the dinner is at 6:00. Let's go to the

dinner together, then I can have you back for your 8:00 date," he suggested.

I couldn't have chosen a better man for my daughter, but she made the choice. I just made the first suggestion. Billy and Anita were one of the first couples to be married in our new church's sanctuary.

I really enjoyed working with Anita and Billy and having them on Briarwood's staff. I was very disturbed when Anita told me she and Billy were praying about moving to Arizona to start a PCA church. I didn't want them to go. We needed them at Briarwood, and Arizona was too far away for them to take *my* grandchildren.

After about a year of praying and interviewing for a position, Nita told me they had decided to go. The committee who had interviewed them really wanted Billy to come out there. "Yeah, I'm sure they do," I said. "Who wouldn't? But I don't think you should go." I told her my reasons.

Anita had tears in her eyes. "Daddy, this has been very hard on me, too. Will you come over and read my journal and the letters Billy has received. Then tell me if you still think God hasn't called us."

The next morning at seven o'clock, I was knocking on Anita's door. We sat down on the couch together, and I read her journal entries.

"*Lord,*" she had written, "*what about my children? I want them to be able to go to Briarwood School. There is so much for them in Birmingham. What will happen to my kids if we go so far away?*"

She had asked God this question then waited quietly asking Him to answer her. "Daddy," she said, "I've never done this before. I usually study a book of the Bible or a topic, and the Lord speaks to me through what I'm studying. But this time I asked Him to show me *specifically* from His Word."

The Scripture God gave her was Isaiah 29:23. "When they see among them their children, the work of my hands, they will keep my name holy; they will acknowledge the holiness of the Holy One of Jacob, and will stand in awe of the God of Israel."

The next journal entry Anita had asked, "*Where is Arizona? It's right by Mexico. Lord, will we have to learn another language?*"

The Scripture Ezekiel 3:5, 6 came to her mind. She looked it up and read, "You are not being sent to a people of obscure speech ... and difficult language whose words you cannot understand."

Then Nita pulled out of her journal several letters Billy had received from friends. One friend wrote he had been impressed by the Lord to send Billy the devotion he had worked on that morning. It was a passage from Genesis 12:1, "Leave your country, your people and your father's household and go to the land I will show you."

There were many other letters they had received saying, "God has to take a leader out of his home town." Another said, "Peter had to step out of the boat on faith."

Nita looked at me. "Daddy, I laughed in my heart when they first asked us to go to Arizona. I thought, *I know God wouldn't ask us to do that.* When we went to the interview out there, we were very nervous. Arizona looked so different from the lush woods and hills of Alabama. We flew into Phoenix, and it looked all brown and dead like a desert.

"The morning before our interview, I got up to spend time with the Lord. I thought, *Why would you bring us here? Why wouldn't you raise up someone who is from Arizona?*

"The Scripture God brought me was Isaiah 35. 'Strengthen the feeble hands, steady the knees that give way; say to those with fearful hearts, Be strong, do not fear; your God will come. The desert and the parched land will be glad; the wilderness will rejoice and blossom. It will greatly rejoice and shout for joy, they will see the glory of the Lord, the splendor of our God. The burning sand will become a pool, the thirsty ground bubbling springs...'"

As I read all these things in her journal, I began to cry. "Truly the Lord is calling you to Arizona. I just didn't want it to be true." I stood up, and we hugged. "What can I do to help you get ready to go?" I asked. If the Lord was calling them, I would never stand in the way.

Billy is now pastoring a rapidly growing church in Scottsdale, Arizona, with Anita and their four children: Taylor, Francie, Richard and Robbie.

I remembered the hard years when Anita, Frank and Peggy were born. They were each fifteen months apart. Frank III had many problems at birth and was in the hospital for several operations as a baby. When he was two, it became apparent that he had lost his hearing. When he was four, he had surgery that corrected it. However, because of his hearing loss, he had trouble with his balance and had to spend many hours in physical and speech therapy.

I remember the late nights working on his homework when he was in school. We didn't want him to be held back a year, because we didn't want him in the same class with Peggy. Everything came naturally for her, and it would be unfair for Frank to have to be in the same grade.

In high school Frank found his niche. He really enjoyed working behind the scenes in technical support. He had a gift for understanding how that complicated machinery worked and excelled in making everything run smoothly.

At the end of his senior year in high school, Briarwood School had an awards ceremony where they handed out certificates for academic honors. Barbara attended and watched as Peggy, who was a junior, won six academic awards. Barbara grew more and more sad and frustrated. It was Frank's senior year and he wasn't getting anything. School had been so hard for him. She thought it wasn't fair!

At the end of the ceremony the principal stood up and made an announcement. "We have always given out honors for academics, but there is a higher award we would like to institute this year. Matthew 20:26 says, 'Whoever wants to become great among you must be your servant and whoever wants to be first must be your slave - just as the Son of Man did not come to be served, but to serve, and to give his life as a ransom for many.'

"This year we are naming a new award honoring what God honors - servanthood. There is a person in the school who has typified servant leadership, and we are honored to present our first annual Christian Servanthood Award..." he paused and smiled, "to Frank Barker III!"

All of a sudden all those academic achievements became empty pieces of paper for Barbara. Tears filled her eyes, and she felt the Lord say to her, "Man looks on the outside of a person, but I look at the heart."

After graduation, sixteen of Frank's friends started an annual banquet at Christmas. Each of them would put a dollar in the "pot" every year. If any of their group got married, they would have to contribute two dollars to the pot the next year. The last one to be married would get the "pot" of money. They envisioned thousands of dollars would go to the "winner."

Beau Miller was the last of the group to be married besides Frank III, and at the Christmas banquet they presented Frank with the "pot." Barbara and I were invited to the celebration and saw Frank presented with a check for $250, much less than the thousands they had envisioned. At the end of the evening, all the guys with Barbara and me gathered around Frank and laid our hands on him. I prayed and asked God to send a wonderful Christian lady for Frank to marry.

Every year Frank, who loved his nieces and nephews, would take them all to the circus. That January he also invited someone else.

Shortly before this, Pam Goff had been in his discipleship group. All her friends had gathered around her and asked God to provide someone special to ask her out on a date.

Frank asked Pam to come to the circus, and she joined our rowdy family for an evening with Barnum and Bailey. Several months later they were married.

Pam is the most wonderful daughter-in-law to Barbara and me. If we had searched the world over, we couldn't have found anyone more perfect for our son.

Hindsight is 20/20. As I look back and see God's hand of guidance in my life, I also see how He has led our children. It is an amazing thing to be led by God. There is nowhere else I would desire to be other than in the center of His guiding will. There is nothing more wonderful for a father and mother to see than their children following the Lord and giving their lives wholeheartedly to Him. "I have no greater joy than this, to hear of my children walking in the truth" (3 John 4, NAS).

Giving away the baby

"My coming to Briarwood would be like Frank trying to play tennis at Wimbledon," was the response one pastor gave our "search committee" when they asked if he would consider being my replacement.

As the days to my retirement grew short, I thought about the early days of the church. I had read how God brought David a band of men to stand and fight with him. I had prayed, "Lord, bring me a band of men who will join hands and be part of this church. Give me a foundation of committed Christian couples to undergird the new thing You are going to do."

Everything great that happened through Briarwood's ministry attests to how God answered this prayer. The church's foundation was not on me, but on the mighty men and women who had joined hands with me to take the gospel out, not only to the city, but the nation and the world.

After forty years, it was time to start planning for my retirement. I had seen fellow pastors suddenly become seriously ill and have to leave their church without a senior minister. Many of those churches went for several years without leadership. I didn't want this to happen to Briarwood so, hoping the transition would go smoother, I stayed until my replacement came on board.

Barbara and I met with some Session members who were in the finance business to figure out how much money we would have to live on. All our married life Barbara had warned, "You can't live this way by giving away your salary. We won't have anything to retire on."

She was right, humanly speaking. All we had was the little we had saved in the PCA's Insurance, Annuities & Retirement fund. However, through the working of the men in the church and the Session, God supplied us a generous retirement. It was such a miracle, we saw again the faithfulness of God. He has always provided all we needed. The greatest gift from the church was paying off all indebtedness on Briarwood's last building. The new pastor would not be burdened with debt.

The congregation elected very capable men and women to serve on the pastoral search committee. They interviewed many excellent men. Some of those interviewed had served at Briarwood as associate pastors. Now they had thriving churches and weren't interested in coming back.

Seventeen years earlier, Briarwood had sponsored a new church in Charlotte, North Carolina, called Christ Covenant Church. A young man named Harry Reeder was selected to be the pastor. He was from Charlotte and had deep roots there.

He had preached at one of our Home Missions Conferences a few years before, and I felt like the Lord was telling me he was to be my replacement. I did not tell this to anyone because I wanted the Lord to lead them, not me.

That little church Harry started had grown to 2,000 members. He told the committee he wasn't interested in leaving Christ Covenant, but would pray and assist them in any way he could.

After interviewing many pastors and traveling to several cities, the search committee concluded that Harry Reeder was the best candidate to pastor Briarwood. Again, he turned them down. He loved his church and didn't think he should leave.

The committee continued to pray and search throughout the PCA. Again they visited Christ Covenant and interviewed Harry and his wife, Cindy. They asked if he would reconsider coming to Briarwood.

Harry said he would pray and ask God if it was His will. The Lord confirmed in his heart that He wanted him to resign as pastor of Christ Covenant and move to Briarwood. It was very difficult for Cindy and him to leave their family, the church they had planted and their newly-built dream home.

God guided Harry through the unanimous vote of the committee and through prayer. He knew the Lord was calling him to take my place. All that was needed then was for the congregation to vote their approval.

Everyone had been praying for the search committee and for God's perfect choice. They were anxious to know who had been chosen. The Session called a congregational meeting to hear the search committee's report and vote on their choice.

I sat on the stage with the committee and looked at the sea of people assembled. Every seat was filled. The anticipation and emotion felt even greater than when we first moved into our new church and worship center.

John Law Robinson, chairman of the search committee, did an outstanding job relating the Lord's unique leading in their choice of Harry and Cindy. When a vote was taken, every member stood. Everyone accepted Harry Reeder as our new pastor.

Harry was installed in the fall of 1999. I moved into the Pastor Emeritus position. My official retirement date was January, 2000. At the "Passing the Mantle" service September 12, 1999, I spoke before installing Harry by reviewing my call to Briarwood.

The following is an excerpt of what I said. It is a commentary on how I have tried to live my life.

In times past God moved in nations to bring mighty awakenings. There were great revivals in England under the ministries of the Wesleys and Whitefield. Here in the United States, God used Jonathan Edward's sermon "Sinners in the Hands of an Angry God" to instigate a great revival. Every 50 to 100 years God has done something dramatic with thousands being converted. I prayed for this kind of revival, and still do, for it is desperately needed.

As I studied John 15, I discovered a continuous revival was available. Jesus said, "I am the vine, you are the branches." If we abide in Him, we will bear fruit, see our prayers answered, experience joy, glorify the Father and give evidence that we are His disciples. Another way of saying "abide in Christ" is "walk in the Spirit," or "live by the Spirit."

The fruit of God's life in us reveals His character, love, joy, peace, patience, kindness, goodness, faithfulness, gentleness and self-control. And the Holy Spirit in us makes an impact upon other people when we share the gospel.

There are four things we do to experience continuous revival. First, we must constantly rely upon Him. We are in the "Vine" when we trust Jesus' death for the forgiveness of our sins and surrender our will to Him as our Master. But we must rely upon Him *daily* to change us and produce His fruit through us.

The second requirement is we must *constantly* relinquish *our* will to *His* will. This is not hard when we remember God is good. He wants the best for us, His children. We make an initial surrender and then daily give up our will for His as He shows us areas of our lives where we might be resisting Him.

Third, we must constantly retain His Word by daily reading and memorizing it. God's Word will transform us as we look at life from His point of view. If we don't know any better, we can't do any better. For this reason we need to understand His ways so we can obey His Word.

The joy of having our prayers answered comes by constantly requesting. The fourth requirement is: we must pray constantly. If enough people in the church constantly rely (or abide), relinquish their wills, retain His Word and make requests to the Lord, then we will have revival. Of course we want nationwide revival and statewide revival, but we can personally see revival in our individual lives as we practice the principles of abiding.

I resolved that this would be my approach to building a church. I would teach the Scriptures until everyone knew how to abide in Christ. My main job as a pastor was to help the members develop and use their gifts, be grounded in the Word, and learn to share their faith.

Paul advised Timothy to "Preach the Word ... correct, rebuke and encourage ... with great patience and careful instruction ... keep your head in all situations, enduring hardship, do the work of an evangelist, discharge all the duties of your ministry." That is how I approached the work of the ministry. I sought to do it, and I've done it very imperfectly. You, my congregation, have been very patient and helped me immensely.

Many emotions affect men who retire, and I was no different. Barbara asked me, "Are you sad that you have now turned over our 'baby' to another man?"

"Yes, I am sad," I admitted. Through our forty years, we had some very good associate ministers. Most of them stayed a few years until they received a call from another church. Briarwood was not their life and blood, but a job. Barbara and I birthed the church and it was as dear to us as our precious children. I guess that was what made it so hard for Barbara when I retired. It tore her up to give up our "child."

I had never let my emotions influence my life, except in my love for Barbara. I told her, "Honey, our job was to see God take Briarwood and move it under the new pastor and keep it moving right on up. He still has a plan for us, and I don't intend to 'retire' from serving Him. It will just be in a different way now. Take a look at my schedule. There are worldwide opportunities God is already opening up. He still has work for us to do. You will be able to continue teaching and speaking and directing the ballet school as you have always done."

"Frank, you know I have begged God to change me from being so emotional. I can't just say, I won't think that way and do it. This is really difficult for me to give up the church."

I hugged her, "I'm glad you don't bottle up your emotions, Sweetheart. God gave them to you, and you don't need to deny them."

"Yes, He did, but I feel like the woman Stuart Brisco described as having a speck of intellect floating on a sea of emotion. I am about to drown in that sea," she confessed.

Most of Barbara's Christian life had been spent on building Briarwood's ministries. When we retired she was depressed. Billy and Nita moved the same year which was a double whammy.

Barbara felt like God was asking her, "Do you really want to build my kingdom or yours?" It was a humbling experience, but a real time of growth and brokenness that drew her closer to God than ever before. A whole volume of poetry was born from her devotions during this time.

Throughout the years, I have traveled thousands of miles overseas and been in nearly every state preaching and teaching. The good thing is that now, Barbara sometimes goes with me. In 2001, I was gone 141 days preaching or teaching in 55 events. During the school year she stays busy with the ballet, speaking and teaching at least five Bible classes a week. That keeps her from being lonely with me gone so much.

My heart's vision continues to be for the building of God's kingdom from Birmingham to the ends of the world. One of my great frustrations is that, although I can grow disciples, despite all my noble efforts, I cannot grow grass in our yard!

That boy made a good pastor

Writing the life story of Frank Barker has been a process of "slash and burn." So much material that could, and probably should, be included was left out. There is no way to record all the great things God has done in and through him. Therefore, I have written about the man and not his voluminous accomplishments. After two years of collecting information and praying, God led me to write as if Frank was telling his own story.

Humble was the word that kept surfacing from people who know Frank's character and the mighty things God did through him. Few pastors in this generation had the vision like Frank's to reach people for Jesus Christ. His motto for the church was "Worshiping God and Equipping Christians to reach Birmingham to Reach the World for Christ." When he retired, there were 4,000 church members and 105 different ministries reaching from the inner city to the medical and business men and women, and the internationals living in Birmingham.

Campus Outreach was started to reach students on the small universities and colleges. Presently, there is staff on fifty-four campuses including several overseas.

We never referred to him as Reverend or Doctor Barker even after he received two honorary doctorates. Reformed Theological Seminary bestowed upon him the only honorary doctorate they have ever given. He received another doctorate from Knox Seminary. To his congregation, he was and is, simply Frank. At the graveside of Elizabeth Newbold, a famous Bible teacher in Alabama, he said in great humility, "This lady taught me the ministry of the Holy Spirit."

Frank loved his flock and *protected* them from error. One of the many ways he did this was reading every book offered in the church's bookstore. Yet, he was willing to share his people with other pastors who were starting a church. He would introduce the young pastors from the pulpit and say, "He is starting a new church, and any of you who are led, join him and help establish this church."

Hundreds of churches have been *revived* and become strong mission-giving churches through his influence and teaching. It's worth mentioning again that he was one of the "fathers" of the PCA.

Frank was always *available* to his congregation. His home telephone did not have an answering machine. He frequently answered his office phone when his secretary was busy.

He *supported* by his presence and advice every good evangelical meeting or outreach in Birmingham. He *encouraged* young men starting out in the ministry. Summer interns were given a chance to lead church services and fill in for his Bible classes. Sandy Wilson, pastor of Second Presbyterian Church in Memphis, Tennessee, wrote, "Frank grabbed my arm at a meeting and asked, 'Hey, Sandy, tell me how you're doing?' At that time, I could not imagine how Frank could possibly have remembered my name. He was always careful to build up young men. Frank has been incredibly accessible and consistently supportive of me and my ministry. Had it not been for his blessing, I probably would never have come to Second Presbyterian in Memphis."

He was committed to *teaching the Word of God.* The Birmingham Theological Seminary that he and Bill Hay, pastor at Covenant Presbyterian, started has given opportunity for men and women in ministry to receive further training. Laymen and women also take courses and find the classes change their lives. One forty-six-year-old student wondered why it took him so long to realize his need for knowledge of God's Word. A pastor wrote about his studies and said they caused him to "fall in love again with my call to the ministry." The Dean of Women at a Bible college said her studies at the seminary "provided me with abundant material and superb background for addressing particular issues" that came up in classes she taught.

The BTS is a non-profit Alabama corporation and an independent, reformed, evangelical seminary. It has branches in Tuscaloosa, Montgomery, Greensboro and Eutaw, Alabama, and one in the Birmingham Easonian Baptist Bible College. There are three ways to study a course: live classes, taped courses and directed studies.

Frank was broken to the will of God, chosen, called and guided each step of his way by our great God and Father of the Lord Jesus Christ. He kept right on doing what God called him to, even though it may not always have been the easiest or most popular thing to do. Difficulties never deterred him. He is an example to follow.

Frank was a marked man from the beginning. Once God called him, he never swerved or looked back. He could say to us what Paul said to Timothy, "You follow my teaching, conduct, purpose, faith, patience, love, perseverance, persecutions and sufferings..." His teaching was always "Thus saith the Lord."

As I have written about his life and recorded it on these pages, my life has been greatly influenced. I hope that yours will be also.

That boy made a good pastor.

Supernatural Living for Natural People

Studies in Romans 8

Raymond C. Ortlund Jr

Romans 8 is a favorite of many Christians. It opens up to us peace with God, the ministries of the Spirit, the urgency of personal reformation, the glory of our eternal inheritance, the power of God's goodness at work in our daily lives and the invincibility of his loving intentions toward us.

'This is a choice study of the eighth chapter of Romans by an outstanding scholar and gifted expository preacher. Dr. Ortlund mines the depths of this chapter, but what he produces is a book of such practical and spiritual riches as we seldom read today.'

Eric Alexander

'Ray Ortlund in his exposition of Romans 8 has succeeded in weaving together both truth and application, both theology and the realities of everyday life. He shows that Romans 8 speaks to many of our deepest needs, such as the need for forgiveness, power, assurance, and security.'

**Tom Schreiner,
Southern Baptist Seminary, Louisville, Kentucky**

'There is meat for the hungry soul here. There is refreshing water for the thirsty spirit. Ray's confidence in the power of the Spirit-energized Word of God shows forth on every page of this wonderful, Christ-exalting study of Romans 8. Get it. Then let it get you!'

Dr. Sam Storms, Wheaton College

Raymond C. Ortlund Jr. serves as Senior Minister at First Presbyterian Church, Augusta, Georgia.

ISBN 1 85792 694 3

Preparing your Church for Revival
T.M. Moore

We all long for revival, but we tend to pray for it to come without being completely sure what precisely revival is. This book will be a revitalising aid to those of us who desire revived spiritual life for our churches. T.M. Moore offers practical advice on steps, each with secure scriptural foundations, that we can take to prepare our churches for the sovereign work that is revival. This book is clear that there is no conflict between revival being a work of God and the continued and urgent need for God's people to earnestly pray for its appearance.

With practical guides to prayer for revival T.M. Moore realises the need for balance and succeeds in providing a book that will help us to refocus on revival, and will prepare our souls and our churches for the mighty work of a Sovereign and loving God.

'Think of T. M. Moore's work as high-octane fuel, written by a man who loves the church of Jesus Christ and longs to see her full of his glory once again. I pray his 'fuel' will ignite churches with longing for a true visitation of God in our time.'
John Armstrong, President, Renew, Illinois

T. M. Moore is Pastor of Teaching Ministries at Cedar Springs Presbyterian Church in Knoxville, TN. His most recent book is *A Mighty Fortress* (1 85792 868 7). He and his wife, Susie, have four children and nine grandchildren.

ISBN 1 85792 698 6

....of Such is the Kingdom
Nurturing Children in the Light of Scripture
Dr. Timothy A. Sisemore

Are you, and your church, bringing up children the way God wants you to?

Timothy Sisemore builds a practical approach to parenting and children's ministry and shows how to nurture children to be disciples. This is not a theoretical book - if you recognise the need to change your approach he shows you how to do that too.

'Here is a straightforward, readable, challenging and practical manual - just what parents are looking for.'
Sinclair B. Ferguson

'underscores the need not only to teach our children about God but also to develop a worldview that enables them to see the totality of their Christian faith in all things....I will recommend it as an important book.'
Charles Dunahoo, Christian Education & Publications, Presbyterian Church in America (PCA)

'His approach is what the Bible calls wisdom...as rich in Biblical instruction as it is in psychological insight.'
**Edmund P. Clowney,
Westminster Theological Seminary**

Timothy A. Sisemore, Ph.D. is Academic Dean and Associate Professor of Counseling at the Psychological Studies Institute in Atlanta and Chattanooga. He is married to Ruth and they have one daughter, Erin.

ISBN 1 85792 514 9

My Flesh and my Heart may Fail
Life on the Edge of Open Heart Surgery
Margaret Carroll Lamkin

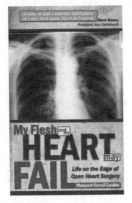

How would you react to the threat of losing your life?

At one point Margaret's heart had lost over 88% of its ability to function. Blood fungus infections and fevers were dragging her down further – an urgent call went out for prayer. The result was described by her doctor as 'a miracle'.

Margaret Lamkin's story is a gutsy, heart-churning chronicle told with warmth and insight. It will help you understand how God can work through the challenges you will face in your life

"...a story of God's absolute faithfulness in a very dark place. You'll be inspired"
Steve Brown, President, Key LifeNetwork

'At one point or another all of us face trials in life that challenge our faith. We can all find hope and inspiration in the pages of Margaret's story.'
Richard Pratt, Reformed Theological Seminary

'I have known Margaret since she was a student/teacher for Inter-Varsity Christian Fellowship. My first prayer, when I received the note requesting prayer during the severe trauma that she went through was, "Lord, why?" This book tells you why God makes no mistakes.'
Harry L. Reeder III, Briarwood Presbyterian Church

Margaret Lamkin is a pastor's wife and Children's Therapist from Jacksonville, Florida
ISBN 1 85792 643 9

When Grace Transforms

*the character of Christ's disciples
envisioned in the beatitudes*
Terry L. Johnson

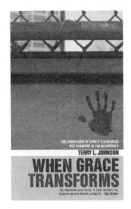

*My "Sermon on the Mount' note book
is now crammed with Johnson-isms
- pithy one-liners that get to the heart
of what Jesus meant by adorning the
righteousness of the kingdom of God.
This is where preaching and teaching
needs to go.'*

**Derek W. H. Thomas
Reformed Theological Seminary,
Jackson, Mississippi**

*'...shows us here a picture of what
transforming grace looks like in the*
life of a believer, and he does so following Jesus' own description
of his disciples in the Beatitudes. What a timely emphasis for a
generation long on license and short on character.'

**J. Ligon Duncan III
First Presbyterian Church, Jackson, Mississippi**

'...a clarion call to discipleship in depth.'

**J. I. Packer
Professor of Theology, Regent College, Vancouver**

Terry explains each of the beatitudes, showing both **what
they don't mean, and what they do**. His conclusions are
strong, challenging, and immensely practical.

Let Jesus change your attitudes

Terry Johnson is the senior pastor of the Independent Presbyterian Church in Savannah, Georgia.

ISBN 1 85792 770 2

Christian Focus Publications

publishes books for all ages.

Our mission statement –

STAYING FAITHFUL

In dependence upon God we seek to help make his infallible word, the Bible, relevant. Our aim is to ensure that the Lord Jesus Christ is presented as the only hope to obtain forgiveness of sin, live a useful life and look forward to heaven with him.

REACHING OUT

Christ's last command requires us to reach out to our world with his gospel. We seek to help fulfil that by publishing books that point people towards Jesus and for them to develop a Christ-like maturity. We aim to equip all levels of readers for life, work, ministry and mission.

Books in our adult range are published in three imprints.

CHRISTIAN HERITAGE contains classic writings from the past.

MENTOR focuses on books written at a level suitable for Bible College and seminary students, pastors, and other serious readers; the imprint includes commentaries, doctrinal studies, examination of current issues and church history.

CHRISTIAN FOCUS contains popular works including biographies, commentaries, basic doctrine and Christian living. Our children's books are also published in this imprint.

For a free catalogue of all our titles, please write to:
Christian Focus Publications, Ltd
Geanies House, Fearn, Tain, Ross-shire,
IV20 1TW, Scotland, United Kingdom
info@christianfocus.com

For details of our titles visit us on our website
www.christianfocus.com